Programming in POP-11

Artificial Intelligence Texts

Artificial Intelligence Texts

Programming in POP-11

JONATHAN LAVENTHOL
Director
GLH Limited
7 Old Steine
Brighton BN1 1EJ

Blackwell Scientific Publications
OXFORD LONDON EDINBURGH
BOSTON PALO ALTO MELBOURNE

© Jonathan Laventhol 1987
Blackwell Scientific Publications
Editorial offices:
Osney Mead, Oxford OX2 0EL
  (*Orders*: Tel. 0865 240201)
8 John Street, London WC1N 2ES
23 Ainslie Place, Edinburgh EH3 6AJ
52 Beacon Street, Boston
  Massachusetts 02108, USA
667 Lytton Avenue, Palo Alto
  California 94301, USA
107 Barry Street, Carlton
  Victoria 3053, Australia

POPLOG is a trademark of the University of
  Sussex.
VAX, PDP and VMS are trademarks of Digital
  Equipment Corporation.
Apple and Macintosh are trademarks of Apple
  Computer, Inc.
Atari is a trademark of Atari, Inc.
IBM is a trademark of International Business
  Machines Corporation.
Unix is a trademark of AT&T.

First published 1987

Set by V & M Graphics Ltd, Aylesbury, Bucks
Printed and bound in
Great Britain by
Billing and Sons Ltd., Worcester

DISTRIBUTORS

USA and Canada
  Blackwell Scientific Publications Inc
  P O Box 50009, Palo Alto
  California 94303
  (*Orders*: Tel. (415) 965-4081)

Australia
  Blackwell Scientific Publications
  (Australia) Pty Ltd
  107 Barry Street
  Carlton, Victoria 3053
  (*Orders*: Tel. (03) 347 0300)

British Library
Cataloguing in Publication Data

Laventhol, J.
  Programming in POP-11.
  1. POP-11 (Computer program language)
  I. Title
  005.13'3   QA76.73.P/

ISBN 0-632-01736-8
ISBN 0-632-01528-4 Pbk

Library of Congress
Cataloguing-in-Publication Data

Laventhol, J. (Jonathan), 1961–
  Programming in POP11.
  Includes index.
  1. POP11 (Computer program language)
  I. Title.
QA76.73.P65L38   1987   005.13'3   87-16654

ISBN 0–632–01736–8

Dedicated to Helen, who has mastered the trick
of getting younger as the years go by: happy birthday

Contents

Foreword

POP-11 is one of the finer programming languages, and is becoming more popular as more people use it. It has been with us, in various forms, for some 18 years. Compared with modern POP-11, the original language reads like old English. But in that time, very few of the core strengths of the language have changed, a great tribute to its designers.

The language is named after one of them, Robin Popplestone, whose languages POP-1 and POP-2 were the ancestors of POP-11. In his 1968 paper 'The Design Philosophy of POP-2' he presented a Bill of Rights for data objects, which, translated into current POP-11 terminology, is this:

All objects have certain fundamental rights.

1. All objects can be the arguments of procedures.
2. All objects can be returned as results of procedures.
3. All objects can be the subject of assignment statements.
4. All objects can be tested for equality.

One of the key features of the language has been the careful attention to efficiency the designers have put in. It is usual to mention first the language's pedigree in artificial intelligence research, but one of the purposes of this book is to promote the use of POP-11 in other areas, where efficiency is keenly watched.

AI applications have always demanded the most in terms of expressive power from the software and computational might from the hardware. POP-11 is a practical implementation of an extremely clean and clear language. Its continued use and development in the research institutes of this and other countries testifies to that.

The fact that it copes easily with AI research problems would perhaps lead people to suspect it wasn't suited to more mundane programs such as screen editors, payroll packages and file manipulating programs. But its popularity for these kinds of tasks in the places where it was made available for other purposes shows the breadth of its application.

Being an interactive language, the debugging loop is extremely brief, saving many hours of programmer time. Modern implementations are either incrementally compiled to native code, or partially compiled and then interpreted. Both methods are fast: the incremental compiler will become the standard method for interactive languages; it is already standard in POP-11.

One of the places in which POP-11 comes into its own is compiler writing. In tasks such as experimenting with a new language, POP-11 has one of the best testbeds available. Usually, the internal compilation process is available to the user, through a virtual machine interface, which is extremely easy to compile into. There are many experimental languages in use which have been built in exactly this way. There are many PROLOG and LISP systems written in POP-11, from students' term projects through to full commercial implementations.

The dominant implementation of POP-11 is that found in the POPLOG system of the University of Sussex, which was originally developed to run on Digital's VAX minicomputer range, and has since been expanded for large 68000-family microcomputer systems running Unix. This system has online documentation, screen editors, windowing systems, PROLOG, Common LISP, Object-Oriented Programming systems and many other things it would takes pages to describe. All user code is incrementally compiled into host machine code.

A smaller system, ALPHA POP-11, which runs on the Apple Macintosh, has been implemented by Cognitive Applications Limited. This should bring the language to many more users than was possible before, and is highly compatible with POPLOG POP-11. The system compiles into an intermediate representation which is then interpreted. Cognitive Applications plans to release the system on other hosts, such as IBM PC and Atari.

Implementations for other systems can be expected as the language gets more established in the academic institutions, and the expertise filters into the commercial sector. POP-11 is not a difficult language to implement – there are half a dozen or so small implementations in commercial companies, written mainly for experiment.

The purpose of this book is to present the language in a simple manner, suitable for people who have some training in computer languages who want to learn POP-11; those who have some knowledge of POP-11 but want more; or those starting completely from scratch, preferably as part of a course. It should form a good basis for undergraduate courses in programming, whether from arts or science backgrounds.

No understanding of mathematics is assumed, although there are some mathematical exercises for those who want them. No detailed knowledge is required of machine details, either, although there is some detailed description of the compilation process, and the actual executed code, for those who are interested. Readers are asked to skip the parts which they find are unintelligible without being too scathing of the author.

Acknowledgements

Thanks are due:

To Mike Greenwell, now of Expert Systems International, for the many conversations and cups of coffee which got this book going.

To my friends and ex-colleagues at the University of Sussex who made POP-11 what it is today. Special thanks are due to Aaron Sloman and John Gibson. John is the great unsung hero of POP-11, and one of the most inspiring people I've ever had the pleasure to work with.

To Alex Morrison, Gilly Furse, and their team at Cognitive Applications, for coming up with invaluable criticisms and comments and for the loan of a Macintosh and a beta test version of ALPHA POP-11 to try examples on. Ben Rubinstein deserves a special mention, for the rigorous grilling he gave to some of the later drafts.

To Dominic Vaughan and Bernard Watson at Blackwell Scientific Publications.

To Jane Fordham for the cover drawing: now we all know what foo and baz look like.

Finally, to everyone at GLH for not shouting at me when I took some time off to finish this book; Juliet, Chris, and Hilary for general advice about writing books; everyone who read drafts and made their invaluable comments. And apologies for not making as much of some of their ideas as might have been hoped for: any problems which remain are my fault entirely. I would of course be grateful to hear of any mistakes readers might find.

CHAPTER 1

First Steps

First, an introduction to POP-11, to give perspective. Then a little about how to get your system running. Then on with the code.

Introduction to POP-11

It is helpful to put POP-11 in perspective with the other programming languages about, of which there are a great number. To begin, then, an overview of some of the problems and solutions of more conventional computer systems.

Programming languages are often classified by their 'level'. We frequently hear the term 'high level language'. What does this mean? Apart from its use in advertising hyperbole, it refers to the distance between the program and the underlying architecture of the computer. Currently, all the computers in common use have a very similar architecture, known as the *Von Neumann architecture*. It was named so by John Backus, who characterised the current style of machine as a processor connected to some memory by a pipe – the Von Neumann bottleneck – which greatly restricts the altering of the memory. Data has to flow, a drop at a time, through the pipe, backwards and forwards: like painting your front room through your letterbox.

One of the features of this style of machine is that it can only deal with very impoverished instructions. This means that to do anything useful, many of these instructions must be used. Also, there is very little structure inherent at this level of the machine, and so very intricate and complicated programs can be written. This level is called the *machine code* of the particular machine. In general, different machines have different machine codes, although they tend to be broadly very similar.

This level is the lowest level at which programmers have access to the computer, although system designers sometimes implement the machine code as a program of microinstructions, which are even more primitive. The machine code resides in the memory of the computer, and is normally represented by a series of numbers.

The next level up is *assembler language*. Here, the programmer writes instructions in textual form, and uses a program called an *assembler* to convert them to the final form – the big pile of numbers. In practice, very few people write machine code proper, so the two terms assembler and machine code tend (rightly) to be a little blurred. An assembly language is characterised by the direct correspondance of assembler instructions to machine instructions.

1

It follows from this that the assembly language of different machines is different. This is a real problem, because programs won't be portable across machines. Also, assembler programs are long and complicated, because each problem has to be broken down into such small pieces in order for it to be executed on the machine.

So, higher level languages were developed in order to write programs more easily and more clearly. Programs were developed to make the computer accept the textual form of the language and convert it to a form usable by the computer. Typically, there is a very complex relationship between an instruction in the higher level language and the series of machine code which gets executed for it.

Perhaps the most spectacular characteristic of assembler programs is their ability to go wrong with few or no symptoms appearing. Typical behaviour of such a program running amok includes random characters appearing on screens, or no response whatsoever, requiring that the computer be reset. (Or the program might be halted by the operating system, in a multiuser system.)

In a high level language, we expect better behaviour. Programs should be unable to run away without our being able to get them back and stay in control. We expect to be able to express the program in a clear and concise way. And we expect good reports from the language about any problems which might be in our programs.

As is predictable, there are benefits the other way too. Lower level languages often allow constructions which can save great amounts of time, or offer facilities which are necessary for some kinds of program. So, people who write operating systems often use the C language, as it allows very concise instructions for operations common in such systems. But C lacks some of the safety features described above. FORTRAN is often used because of its numeric processing features, but it lacks some of the structure needed by today's programming techniques.

So – where does POP-11 sit amongst these? Syntactically it is highly structured (like PASCAL, C). It offers a full set of safety features, so bugs in programs can't propagate away from the problems. And it has very powerful primitives which keep programs small and readable.

Getting into POP-11

POP-11 is available on quite a number of different systems, from the small to the large. The most popular implementation is POPLOG, from the University of Sussex, but there are others which have been made in universities and commercial companies. A particularly interesting development is a version of POP-11 to run on Macintosh computers from Cognitive Applications, which also plans to release a version for IBM microcomputers, and Atari ST machines.

The first problem is to get POP-11 going. On the Macintosh, it is as simple as switching on and clicking at an icon.

POPLOG runs on minicomputers and large microprocessor systems. These machines all run Unix (or a derivative); in addition, it runs on VAXes running VMS. Assuming your machine actually has a POPLOG system on it, you may have to talk to your systems manager in order to have the proper access to it.

If you have a terminal in front of you, and you've logged in or switched on as appropriate, you should be able to type **pop** to the operating system, and the system should start. Here's what it looks like on a Unix system:

```
login: slymo
password: XXXXXXX

Welcome to GLH VAX B
% pop11
Sussex POPLOG (Version 12.0 22 June 1987 12:29)

Setpop
:
```

On your system all the messages will probably be a bit different, but the gist of it should be the same. What's happening here is that Slymo is getting access to the computer by identifying himself with his name and password, and then gives the pop11 command.

Below POPLOG's banner is the POP-11 prompt: a colon. In this book examples and snippets of terminal sessions are shown with the prompt, as it will look on the screen. Don't type the colons yourself.

A tiny program just to boost your confidence: type in the following couple of lines. Don't forget to press return at the end of each line, and don't type the colons.

```
: define yes();
:    [yes] =>
: enddefine;
: yes();
```

If you typed it right, it'll print this:

```
** [yes]
:
```

The next thing you'll need to know is how to leave POP-11. Again, this differs on different systems. The Macintosh version has a pop-down menu. The others are harder.

On VMS, you'll have to type control-Z. On some Unix systems it's control-Z, others control-D. Try them. If it doesn't work, get help from someone, or ask your systems manager. After getting out of POP-11 you will normally have to log out of the system. Your system ought to be pretty much like the Unix example:

```
: ^Z
% logout
Goodbye from GLH VAX B
login:
```

And then the system is waiting for the next person.

Overview of POP-11

What is POP-11 like? In a nutshell, it is interactive, it has structure like PASCAL, with storage allocation like LISP, and argument passing like FORTH.

POP-11 has rich structure. The syntax is based on blocks, each of which has matching opening and closing keywords. So if there is a kind of block which begins with the keyword **goo**, the closing keyword will be **endgoo**. We've already seen **define** and **enddefine** a few pages back. At a finer level, the text is broken into items, and the laying out is arbitrary, so the text can be put into whatever shape is convenient.

The basic functional unit is called the *procedure*. There are a great number of procedures which come built-in, and the users' programs consists of their own procedures. There is no difference between built-in and user-defined procedures.

There are many basic data types from very simple to very complex. The simplest type is probably numeric, but there are the usual vectors and arrays. For cleanliness, there are booleans to represent truth and falsehood. Most significantly, however, there are also lists of the same kind as in LISP and PROLOG.

Actually, procedures are also just another kind of data structure, and can be manipulated and passed around as easily as any other data structure.

The most significant thing about the data structures is that they are built when needed while the program is running. This means that programs need never worry about how much space to allocate for some resource. This contrasts sharply against most other programming languages. The system looks after all the memory management, and has a process called *garbage collection* to clean up whenever needed.

POP-11 is a loosely-typed language. This means two important things: firstly, procedures do not have to restrict their arguments and results to being of a single type. Secondly, the elements of, for example, an array do not all have to be of the same type. This is extremely significant. It means that when designing a program, we can match the representation in the program very closely to the object it represents. It also means we can use the same procedures for manipulating different kinds of object. A consequence of this is that POP-11 won't be able to tell the type of an object merely by noting where it came from, and so a hidden portion of each object is used just to describe what kind of object it is.

All data, on its way from A to B, passes through a holding bay called the *stack*. This stack is just like the one in FORTH, except that programs can find out what kind of object each item is as it comes out of the stack, rather than relying on the structure of the program, as in FORTH. The stack works like this: you can push objects onto it, and pop them back off later. The first object on is the last object off. Most of the time, the operation of the stack is not something which needs thinking about. However, a good understanding of it is an important part of understanding POP-11.

A Word About Mishaps

There is no way out of it: programmers make mistakes. What to a human is a typing mistake is a perfectly good, but different, word to POP-11. What looks like a good program written out might not run because of some infinite loop. And then, of course, there are harder problems.

When POP-11 detects something which it can't cope with, it gives a 'mishap' message. (The philosophy behind the name is that together, the human and POP-11 have a problem. The more conventional 'error' message might be taken to suggest that it is entirely the human's fault.) Suppose we had typed in some POP-11, but missed out a semicolon somewhere it was needed – a common enough occurrence. POP-11 would print a message like this:

```
;;; MISHAP: missing separator (eg, semicolon)
;;; INVOLVING: ) hello
;;; DOING: compile
```

The exact form might vary a little, and there might be a lot more information than this. The intent here is to give you as much information as possible about what the problem is and where POP-11 found it, so that you have a good chance to find and then fix the problem quickly.

The first line of the message is a text intended to tell you what kind of problem was found. In this case is says that a separator was missing, perhaps a semicolon. There are several kinds of separators of which semicolons and commas are the most common. The second line gives some of the data which had the problem. In this case these are the text items which were being compiled. The idea in this case is that the semicolon is probably required between these two items. The third line is a indication of what POP-11 was doing when the problem was found. Here, it was running the procedure called compile, which means it was compiling something.

Usually there is more than one thing printed after DOING:, like this:

```
DOING: < foo
```

This means that the problem was found by < (the less-than comparison procedure) when it was running in the procedure foo. So, in this case, you would examine the procedure foo for problems.

Don't worry about getting mishaps – everybody does. And don't worry that they print so much out, POP-11 is just trying to be helpful, it's not shouting at you.

After printing the mishap message, POP-11 sets everything back to normal and stops running your program. Whenever it does this aborting of the program, it prints a message:

Setpop
:

The setpop is there to tell you everything is under control again. You can then try to fix the problem, which might just mean you have to type your command again, but spelt right.

The Data Types

POP-11 has a rich and varied set of data types, which are extendable by the user. This book will deal with only the more generally useful of them – both because they are sufficient to deal with most programming problems, and because some POP-11 implementations do not have the more esoteric types.

POP-11's structures are uniform. That is, everything which POP-11 can deal with is represented in terms of the same structures. This connection may be hard to see at first, but later chapters will tie the links closer between them.

In this section the four most useful types are presented: words, numbers, lists, and booleans. Even with just these, POP-11 has sufficient expressing power for complex tasks.

The following descriptions of the types are structural, not syntactic. The important thing is to understand what the objects are, and therefore what they can represent in your programs. The next section describes the syntax, and has some practical building and printing of the objects.

Words

Words are actually rather intricate structures, and so this presents a simplified view of them. The subtleties will be introduced later.

A word consists of a sequence of characters which is either

(a) Some alphabetic characters, possibly followed by some numeric or alphabetic characters, or

(b) Some symbolic characters which join up, or

(c) A single symbolic character which can't join up.

Most symbolic characters don't join up. But don't worry about this – the symbolic characters which are needed make sense on the page, and can be remembered from the way POP-11 looks.

Here are some examples:

(a) hello catch22 f111 a1b2c3
(b) —> =>   <>
(c) ,   )   [

And counterexamples:

(a) 24hour (doesn't begin with alphabetic)
(b) ,[{} (don't join up)

Comparisons: POP-11 words are basically the same as LISP atoms and PROLOG non-numeric atoms. Those familiar with other languages will be pleased to know that POP-11 also has the more conventional string data type as well.

Numbers

Numbers can be represented in many ways, both in mathematics and in computer science. POP-11 also has many representations, and different implementations support different kinds. But all support decimals and whole numbers – 'floating point' and 'integers'. But POP-11 deals with the numbers in an intuitive way, and you will not have to worry about the distinctions until you want to.

In ordinary use, little distinction is made between different kinds of numbers. In programming, different representations are used, and this reflects the different ways in which people write numbers down. There are four ways which are common: whole numbers, fractions, decimal, and scientific notation.

They look like this:

$$\frac{720}{2730}$$

720   a whole number (integer)
$\frac{691}{2730}$ a fraction
3.141592 a decimal number
6.023×10^{23} a decimal in scientific notation

Different POP-11 implementations have different representations of numbers. All should be able to cope with the integers and decimals and scientific types shown above, although there will probably be limits on the size of the numbers which can be represented in a particular format. POPLOG POP-11 has a particularly rich set of numeric representations which include the fractions shown above, as well as unlimited precision integers, several accuracies of decimals, as well as complex numbers in various formats. This book is not about numeric processing, so we shall not concern ourselves with different numeric types too deeply.

Lists

Here's where POP-11 really gets going. POP-11 has structures for putting the primitive items together.

Of these, the list is the most used, and the most simple. A list is an ordered sequence of POP-11 objects. 'Sequence' means that a list is one-dimensional, like a row of objects. 'Ordered' means that red, green, blue is different from blue, green, red. A schedule is ordered, while an inventory isn't.

Examples:
A list of words:
   hello there marvin

A list of numbers:
   1 5 61 1385 50521

The real use comes when it is remembered that POP-11 is loosely typed, so we can mix the types of the object in a list, for example, to represent a date:

   28 august 1963

And we can put lists in lists. Unfortunately, this is difficult to show unless we have some syntax. These examples are in proper POP-11 syntax, but the details of it will wait until the next chapter.

A name consisting of four objects (first, middles, surname):

   [helen anne elizabeth utteridge]

A date consisting of three objects (day, month, year):

   [22 june 1987]

A birthday list consisting of two objects (name, date):

   [[helen anne elizabeth utteridge] [22 june 1987]]

The birthday list only has two objects in it: two lists. Don't be confused into thinking that it has seven.

   Comparisons: The POP-11 list is exactly the same as that in LISP and PROLOG.

Booleans

Every program makes comparisons between different objects, and therefore has need to represent truth and falsehood. The classical computer technique is to treat 0 as false, and 1 as true. Some languages use different numbers, maybe 1 and –1.

This technique is ugly, and is prone to making programs more complex and data representation more difficult. POP-11 has a data type boolean: and there are exactly two boolean objects – true, and false. These are used wherever you might find ticks and crosses on paper. They are named after their discoverer, George Boole, a 19th century English logician, and are sometimes called 'truth values'.

They can be used like all the other data types, and are the result of most comparison operations. In practice, booleans don't actually appear explicitly in programs all that much, but the concepts are important because all programs will use them to some degree.

Note: LISP uses the atom t and the empty list ( ) to represent truth and falsehood. These are both quite different to the POP-11 booleans. POP-11 has a word t and an empty list [] as well as the two booleans. LISP programmers should be very careful about their use of the empty list.

Building Some Structures

Having given the structural features of our four basic data types, it is time to make some for yourself. There is no substitute for practice actually at the keyboard.

We will need some places to store various results, and so variables are introduced. They are also important from a practical perspective, because they make the syntax more sensible. Syntax for data construction and procedure application are also introduced.

Variables

POP-11, like most languages, has variables for storing data in. The simplest kind of variable is the global variable, and that is what is presented in this section. In day-to-day practice, global variables are not used very much. This is both because of a methodological bias against them, and for simply practical reasons. In their favour, for the present purpose, they are ideal as they require very little knowledge about POP-11. Local variables are presented when you need to define your own procedures.

The POP-11 variable is of the conventional type – it is simply a named box which has various values which you can change. The name can be anything which is a valid word. In general, variables should have names which conform to the first rule for words in the section above – begins with a letter, and consists entirely of letters and digits. For the present, just use lower case letters.

Making a new variable is pretty easy:

```
: vars mine;
```

You can make several all in one go:

: **vars one two three;**

To set the value of **mine** to 123, POP-11 has an arrow construction, called the assignment arrow. It is formed from the minus sign and the greater-than sign, and there must be a semicolon after the name of the variable:

: **123 -> mine;**

Notice that assignment in POP-11 is left to right, unlike most other languages. This is in keeping with the POP-11 philosophy that the data is more important than its location. Notice also that the symbol for it bears no resemblance to the equals sign, as in too many languages.

If you try assigning to a variable which you haven't declared with a **vars** statement, POP-11 helps out by doing it for you, and prints a message like this:

;;; **DECLARING VARIABLE yours**

All it means is that POP-11 did your **vars** statement for you.

Some comments on variable declaration: because we can use whatever data types we like wherever we like, there is no need to specify the type of a variable – it is untyped. So we could now put a list or a word into the variable which currently holds 123. This contrasts with most other languages.

Having got something into a variable, we should be able to see it again. This is easily done with the printarrow, so called because it is formed from the equals sign and the greater-than sign, like this:

: **mine =>**

POP-11 will print the result like this:

** **123**

The two stars are just adornment.

Syntax

The syntax for POP-11 is straightforward, and is presented informally for the different features.

Data Objects

To build a word, and put it into a variable, we have to type the word in double-quote marks. These are usually called 'word quotes' in POP-11. Here are a few lines you should try:

```
: "hello" -> mine;
: mine =>
** hello
```

It should be clear that the word in quotes is simply the word, while the mine is a variable reference, and gets the current value of the variable. To copy the value of one variable to another is equally simple:

```
: mine -> one;
: one =>
** hello
```

Numbers have no special syntax beyond what has already been shown. Just write them down as you would on paper, bearing in mind a few simple rules: if the number has a decimal point in it, it must have at least one digit on each side. The 'E' notation is allowed, and has the usual meaning: 1.2e4 means take 1.2, and multiply it by 10 four times.

Here are some examples:

```
1234    -12    2.71828    6.023e23    0.5772
```

Lists have simple syntax. A list begins with a bracket (usually called a square bracket), has some objects, and finishes with a closing bracket. This example puts a small list of numbers into a variable:

```
: [0 1 1 2 3 5 8] -> mine;
```

Lists print out like they are written:

```
: mine =>
** [0 1 1 2 3 5 8]
```

The only funny thing about lists is that within the brackets, unquoted words are the words, not the variable values. This is most simple illustrated:

```
: vars hello;
: "elephant" -> hello;
: [1 2 hello] =>
** [1 2 hello]
```

Notice that the list didn't get made as [1 2 elephant] as might have been expected.

To get the value of a variable into a list, use a caret (normally called 'up-arrow'):

```
: [1 2 ^hello] =>
** [1 2 elephant]
```

Booleans have no special syntax of their own. Instead, there are two built-in 'variables' called **true** and **false** which have the boolean objects as their values.

There is no way to write down the boolean objects other than by reference to the built-in variables. (Actually, these are constants, not variables, so you can't lose their values accidentally, or on purpose.)

So, to put a truth value into a variable:

```
: true -> mine;
: false -> hello;
```

POP-11 tries to print objects out in a way which looks sensible. If there isn't a special way of printing them which relates to their syntax, then it prints a construction with angle-brackets. There is no syntax for booleans, so they get the angle-bracket treatment:

```
: mine =>
** <true>

: hello =>
** <false>
```

Finally, here's a typical POP structure, a list representing people and their ages:

```
: vars ages;
: [[jonathan 24] [mike 32] [socrates ^false]] -> ages;
```

This representation allows us to code Socrates' mortality in a clean and elegant way.

Procedure Call

A procedure call is when we get a procedure to run. The syntax for this is much shorter to write than to describe:

```
: length(ages) =>
** 3
```

The call consists of the procedure name, an opening parenthesis (round bracket), the arguments separated by commas, and a closing parenthesis.

So, if foo is a procedure which takes three arguments, we might call it like this:

```
: foo("hello", 12, false);
```

There are also a few infix operators. These are ordinary procedures, except that they have special syntax which makes them look nicer in programs. Usually, their names consist of symbol characters, such as the arithmetic operators + and -. Here's a simple example of these:

```
: 1 + 3 =>
** 4
```

Procedures may have arguments, which are the things which it is to work on, and results, which are the things which it produces. In the previous example, the arguments are 1 and 3, and the result is 4. Procedures can have any number of arguments, including none. (The maximum number may be limited for a given implementation. In practice, it would be an unusual procedure indeed which had more than half a dozen arguments.) Procedures may have any number of results, including none.

Simple Procedures

It is worthwhile to spend a little time trying out simple examples in POP-11, just to get used to the way the language looks, and what the data types are. Here are a few simple procedures which you should try with various arguments.

Arithmetic

POP-11 has the usual set of arithmetic operations, most of which are infix operators, so they go between their arguments, and don't need brackets. Addition and subtraction are done with the obvious + and -, multiplication and division by the conventional * and /. Exponentiation is denoted by **. Round brackets can be used wherever desired for making expressions clearer. Operators have precedence associated with them, in order to disambiguate expressions like 2 + 3 * 4, which could mean either 5 * 4 or 2 + 12. In practice, few people can remember the precedences of the operators, and so you should use brackets wherever the slightest confusion arises. In POP-11, ** has tighter precedence than * and /, which in turn are tighter than + and -. Where two (arithmetic) operators are of the same precedence, evaluation proceeds from left to right. So, our previous example mean the same as 2 + (3 * 4), which is 14.

Try a few examples for yourself. Try to guess the result first, and then compare that with POP-11's answer.

(a) : 3 * 4 + 5 =>
(b) : 10 ** 3 =>

Lists

POP-11 has a great number of procedures for working on lists. A simple one has already been introduced: length. This takes a single list as argument, and returns its length, which is the number of elements it has.

There is nothing complex about finding the length of a list. But there are a few cases which you might try, just to practice the syntax. It is particularly important to become familiar with lists and their syntax, as their use is so ubiquitous in POP-11.

(a) : length([hello there batman]) =>
(b) : length([[hello there batman] =>
(c) : length([[] []]) =>
(d) : length([]) =>
(e) : vars list;
    : [hello robin] -> list;
    : length(list) =>
    : length([list]) =>
    : length([list list]) =>

Words

As brought out in the introduction, there is nothing to stop us writing

: length("hello") =>

or

: "hello" + 3 =>

because we are allowed to pass any type of argument to any procedure. What should happen for these? It would be nice if the first returned 5, the number of characters in "hello". Indeed, this is exactly what happens. But for the second idea, adding a number to a word, it is difficult to think of a rule for what the result should be. In this case, procedures usually cause mishaps. The mishap for this would look like this:

```
MISHAP:    NUMBERS NEEDED
INVOLVING: hello 3
DOING:     + compile
```

The message indicates that the procedure + won't work if you give it things other than numbers.

CHAPTER 2

Basic List Processing

Introduction

This chapter will give you the tools to make lists really work for you. As mentioned earlier, lists really are one of the key features of a language like POP-11. And the key to good programming is getting the data representation right.

Rather than give long-winded instructions on what kinds of things are possible with lists in POP-11, it is preferable to show some real live usage of them. This is for two reasons: to show some POP-11 programming style, and because examples are more readily comprehended.

Building a Useful Structure

Many people use POP-11 for natural language analysis and generation. Given a sentence like this: 'the small cat ate the food', a linguist might want to draw a diagram like that shown in Figure 2.1. The diagram represents the parse tree for the sentence, and shows that it is made of a noun phrase followed by a verb phrase, that the noun phrase is made up of three parts, and so on.

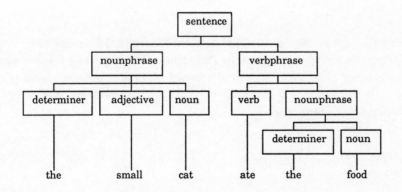

Fig. 2.1

How could this drawing be represented in POP-11? A commonly-used approach gives this list:

```
: vars parse;
: [sentence
:     [nounphrase
:          [determiner the]
:          [adjective small]
:          [noun cat]
:     ]
:     [verbphrase
:          [verb ate]
:          [nounphrase
:               [determiner the]
:               [noun food]
:          ]
:     ]
: ] -> parse;
```

Notice the indentation. As in most languages, good POP-11 programming demands good indentation. For a structure like this, there is very little hope of typing it correctly without the indentation. Notice that the brackets are matched correctly.

How does it represent the tree drawn above? Consider the top-level list. It has three elements. The first is **sentence**, indicating that this list represents a sentence. The two other elements represent the two legs below 'sentence' in the diagram, which are the components of the sentence.

Getting at the Parts

Having made our tree, how do we get at the component parts? There are many ways, and perhaps the simplest is numerical. This technique is sometimes frowned upon because it is not as machine efficient as some of the others, but it is probably the easiest to understand. It must also be said that it is not the most useful method either – that comes later in the chapter.

Consider this:

```
: parse(1) =>
** sentence
```

This should be pretty straightforward. It is a general principle of POP-11 structures that they can be numerically subscripted. Note that the first object has subscript 1, unlike in many other languages.

: parse(2) =>
** [nounphrase [determiner the] [adjective small] [noun cat]]

Don't worry because POP-11 has printed the list differently from what was typed in. The only thing changed is the indentation – it should be clear that there is nothing structurally different.

The last question about numerical subscripting is what happens if the subscript is no good? POP-11 will give an error if the subscript is not a whole number from 1 to the length of the list, and will also mishap if the subscript isn't numeric. Here is a demonstration of this:

: parse(0) =>
;;; MISHAP - INTEGER >= 0 NEEDED
;;; INVOLVING: [sentence [nounphrase [determiner the] [adjective small] [noun cat]] [verbphrase [verb ate] [nounphrase [determiner the] [noun food]]]] 0
;;; DOING: subscrl compile

Two observations come from this: mishap messages can sometimes be ugly and difficult to read, and the DOING part of the message can take some interpreting. subscrl is the procedure which gets run when lists are subscripted. Don't be put off by mishap's poor formatting.

Exercises A

Assume these variables:

: vars hello goodbye;
: [bonjour monsieur poirot] -> hello;
: [au revoir hercule] -> goodbye;

1. What do these expressions print out?
    (a) : hello(1) =>
    (b) : goodbye(3) =>
    (c) : hello(10) =>

2. What expression printed these?
    (a) ** monsieur
    (b) ** au
    (c) MISHAP: SUBSCRIPT OUT OF RANGE
        INVOLVING: [au revoir hercule] 7

Heads and Tails

The reason lists have become so popular in the various systems which offer them is severalfold. One is the philosophy of programming which requires them, complete with automatic storage reclamation and untyped variables. Another reason is that they are inherently efficient where data objects must change length. We are not so concerned with this second aspect, but it is nonetheless useful to have an understanding of the basic construction of lists.

Firstly, there is a special 'empty' list, sometimes referred to as nil. It is written [], which is indicative of its emptiness: it is simply a list with no elements. This is more useful than it may seem. For example, a program which manages payrolls might have a variable which contains of list of people who have already been paid each month. Before anyone has been paid, the list would be empty. POP-11's [] represents this perfectly.

Every non-empty list, of whatever length, consists of two parts, known as the head and the tail of the list. The head is the first element, and the tail is a list of all the rest of the elements.

Here's a short list:

```
: vars l;
: [a b c] -> l;
```

The head of this list is a, and the tail is [b c]. POP-11 has two procedures for taking lists apart in this way, called hd and tl.

```
: hd(l) =>
** a
: tl(l) =>
** [b c]
```

What happens to tl if there are no elements after the first?

```
: tl([a]) =>
** []
```

Which surely makes sense. [] is just a list with no elements, an empty list. What happens to hd and tl when there are no elements at all?

```
: hd([]) =>
;;; MISHAP - NON EMPTY LIST NEEDED
;;; INVOLVING: []
;;; DOING: hd compile
```

: tl([]) =>
;;; MISHAP - NON EMPTY LIST NEEDED
;;; INVOLVING: []
;;; DOING: tl compile

The only list without a head or a tail is []: there is no first element, so hd can't work; and there are no elements after the first, so tl can't work either. Every other list has both a head and a tail. The tail is one element shorter than the original list, and the head is the first item of the original.

Comparison: lists in POP-11 are just the same as lists in PROLOG and LISP. However, the procedures in POP-11 often don't behave exactly the same as corresponding functions in LISP or predicates in PROLOG. POP-11's hd and tl correspond to LISP's car and cdr, and to unifying with [X |_] and [_ |X] in PROLOG. There are some differences in the advanced features of these POP-11 procedures which have no analogue in LISP or PROLOG. Note that in some LISP systems (car ()) and (cdr ()) are both nil.

Exercises B

It is worth saying that good programming demands simplicity of expression. In POP-11, good modular style will almost always obviate long intricate expressions. They are here so that you can check that you understand the principles behind the working of lists. If you can do these exercises, you can work lists as well as anyone. Questions 3 and 4 demonstrate that complicated expressions are very difficult to use – avoid things like this in your programs.

Assume these variables:

: vars birds dogs;
: [parrot canary peacock] -> birds;
: [dalmation yorkie poodle] -> dogs;

1. What do these expressions print?
    (a) : tl(birds) =>
    (b) : hd(dogs) =>
    (c) : hd(tl(tl(birds))) =>
    (d) : tl(tl(tl(dogs))) =>

2. What expressions printed these?
    (a) ** canary
    (b) ** [yorkie poodle]
    (c) ** []
    (d) ** [peacock]

3. Using **parse** from the beginning of this chapter, what do these expressions print?
   (a) : hd(hd(tl(hd(tl(parse))))) =>
   (b) : hd(hd(tl(tl(parse)))) =>

4. Using **parse** from the beginning of this chapter, what expressions printed these?
   (a) ** cat
   (b) ** [ate]

Joining Lists Together

It is often useful to join lists together, and there are many ways to do this. The reason that there are so many ways is because the different methods are appropriate in different circumstances, depending on the objects which the lists are representing.

A New List of Old Elements

Imagine a program which is constructing the parse tree presented earlier. Suppose it has two variables, which for the moment we can construct by hand, like this:

```
: vars np vp;
: [nounphrase
:     [determiner the]
:     [adjective small]
:     [noun cat]
: ] -> np;

: [verbphrase
:     [verb ate]
:     [nounphrase
:         [determiner the]
:         [noun food]
:     ]
: ] -> vp;
```

Now what the program needs to do is join them together as elements of a list, and add the word **sentence** at the front of this new list. Easily done:

```
: vars s;
: [sentence ^np ^vp] -> s;
: s =>
** [sentence [nounphrase [determiner the] [adjective small] [noun cat]]
[verbphrase [verb ate] [nounphrase [determiner the] [noun food]]]]
```

Here we see that the printarrow => has not shown the structure of the list very nicely, but you should be able to identify the parts easily enough. In circumstances like this, it is better to use the'pretty printarrow' ==> which formats structured lists like this to look nice on the screen.

```
: s ==>
** [sentence
  [nounphrase
      [determiner the] [adjective small] [noun cat]]
  [verbphrase
      [verb ate]
      [nounphrase
          [determiner the]
          [noun food]]]]]
```

And the two parts of the parse tree have been joined in the right way to form the tree which represents the sentence.

In general, the up-arrow notation puts the values of variables into the resultant list, as individual elements.

A New List of Another List's Elements

Suppose we have a program which manipulates a database about the House of Commons, which supplies information about MPs. In such a program, there might be a list of Conservative members, and a list of Labour members. In POP-11, a program along these lines might look like this:

```
: vars conservative labour;
: [thatcher tebbit fowler] -> conservative;
: [kinnock healey livingstone] -> labour;
```

At some point in the program, it might be useful just to have a list of all the MPs. We can't use the up-arrow mechanism shown above, because we would get a list with two elements, each a list of MPs. Instead, we want a list of MPs directly. In such circumstances, use the double up-arrow, like this:

```
: vars mps;
: [^^conservative ^^labour] -> mps;
: mps =>
** [thatcher tebbit fowler kinnock healey livingstone]
```

If we had used the single up-arrow, the result would have been quite different. This example should be contrasted with the previous one, as the distinction is important in POP-11 programs:

```
: vars badmps;
: [^ conservative ^ labour] -> badmps;
: badmps =>
** [[thatcher tebbit fowler] [kinnock healey livingstone]]
```

Newcomers to POP-11 often get the single and double up-arrows confused. The two are quite different, and produce lists of completely different structure. Just keep these simple rules in mind:

The single up-arrow ^ introduces the value of a variable as a single element of the new list.

The double up-arrow ^^ introduces the elements of a list in a variable as elements of the new list.

Exercises C

Assume these variables:

```
: vars good bad ugly;
: [a b c] -> good;
: [x y] -> bad;
: [] -> ugly;
```

1. What is printed out for these expressions?
    (a) : [^ good ^^ bad] =>
    (b) : [^^ good ^ bad] =>
    (c) : [^^ good ^^ bad ^^ ugly] =>
    (d) : [^ good ^ bad ^ ugly] =>
    (e) : [^ good [^^ good]] =>
    (f) : [^^ good iguana [^ ugly] aardvark ^^ ugly] =>

2. What expressions printed these?
    (a) ** [x y a b c]
    (b) ** [[] [x y] [a b c]]
    (c) ** [[[x y]]]
    (d) ** [[[a b c]] [x y] x y]
    (e) ** [a b c]
    (f) ** [a b c d e f g]

More Ways to Skin Cats

One of POP-11's strengths is that there is almost always more than one way to acheive any particular action. This is very useful when writing programs, as each way offers its own benefits. A particular aspect which has recognition in POP-11 is that the way the program looks is important. If it is easy to read, programmers will make fewer mistakes, and maintenance is easier.

As lists are ubiquitous in POP-11 programs, there are many ways of achieving the same result. This section shows ways of joining lists which are less flexible than the single and double up-arrows already introduced. However, they may be clearer in individual cases, and some of them offer machine efficiency advantages.

Adding One Element to the Beginning

A common action is adding an element to the beginning of a list, such as in this example:

```
: vars shopping;
: [coffee chocolate cream] -> shopping;
: [cocoa ^^ shopping] -> shopping;
```

Instead of using the double up-arrow technique, there is a special operator called 'cons' for doing this. Syntactically, it is an operator, which means it goes between its arguments. It uses the symbol 'colon-colon' ::, and in the example above, it could replace the last line thus:

```
: "cocoa" :: shopping -> shopping;
```

A point about efficiency: in small examples as have been shown so far, it won't make any significant difference what way things are done. However, if a program is manipulating large lists, things are different. So, if you are adding elements to a list, add them at the front if you can. It makes no real difference whether you use up-arrows or cons, but if you care about efficiency, do try to avoid this:

```
: [^^ shopping bread] -> shopping;
```

Adding Many Elements to the Beginning

In the examples about Members of Parliament, there was this expression:

```
: [^^ conservative ^^ labour] -> mps;
```

POP-11 has another operator, called 'append', which performs exactly this task for two lists. If you need to join more than two lists, the double up-arrow is better. Append is represented by 'less-than-greater-than' <>, and could join the politicians like this:

```
: conservative <> labour -> mps;
```

A point about efficiency: the uses of ^^ and <> shown here are equally efficient. However, if you care about efficiency, put the shorter lists to the left. If our program really listed all the MPs, and if there is a Conservative majority in the House of Commons, then

: labour <> conservative -> mps;

would be quicker than

: conservative <> labour -> mps;

The Virtual Machine and the Stack

All POP-11 objects are manipulated on a stack, known as the 'user stack' or 'argument stack'. This is a simple mechanism for passing objects from one procedure to another, as a temporary holding bay. It is also sometimes used explicitly to manipulate many objects in one go.

POP-11 also has another stack, known as the 'system stack' or 'recursion stack', which keeps track of the order in which procedures have called each other, and maintains other information to do with variables. Normally, the operation of the system stack is completely invisible to the programmer, and there is no way to manipulate it directly. The one place where it is visible is in mishap messages. The information in the DOING message of a mishap is obtained from the system stack. This stack is very rarely referred to, and so talk of the POP-11 'stack' almost always means the user stack.

A stack is a common kind of data structure, often used in programs. It is used where objects need to be remembered and then recovered, and the most recently remembered object is the first to be recovered – sometimes called a *last-in first-out* stack. Putting an object onto the stack is usually called 'pushing', and getting it back is called 'pulling' or 'popping'. So, if we push cat, then push dog, the first object which will be pulled is dog, and then cat. The 'top' of the stack contains the object which was pushed last.

In POP-11, arguments to procedures are pushed onto the user stack, and the procedure pops them when needed. Similarly, results of procedures are pushed onto the stack, and subsequent procedures pop them off as their arguments. As mentioned previously, some programs also use the user stack in other ways.

An example:

: length([cat dog mouse]) =>
** 3

In the beginning, the stack is empty. Then the [cat dog mouse] list is made, and pushed onto the stack. Then the procedure length is called, which pops the list off the stack, does its computation, and pushes its result, 3. Then the printarrow procedure is called, which pops its argument, 3, and prints it out. The printarrow doesn't have a result, and so the stack is empty again.

In common with other programming languages, POP-11 has an underlying 'virtual machine', or VM, which is an imaginary machine for executing the POP-11 code. This is an explanatory tool, for understanding the way the language works. In actual fact, all current POP-11 implementations do translate the programs given them into a representation of the virtual machine code, which is then more easily dealt with by the compiler or interpreter. Translating input through several intermediate internal representations is a common technique, both for language implementations and other programs.

The VM language, or the instructions which the virtual machine can deal with, is very simple. Obviously, in a full-blown implementation such as POPLOG, there are a great many refinements and subtleties in the way this operates. However, the underlying principles are straightforward.

There are a few core virtual machine instructions, dealt with briefly here. This is an explanatory description, and it is likely that any implementation of the virtual machine in a given POP-11 system will differ in many details.

The key elements of the language are pushing objects onto the stack, popping objects from the stack into variables, and calling procedures. There must also be inherent primitives for making the various POP-11 objects, and there must be some way of implementing control loops. And usually, common sequences of VM instructions are also implemented as their own instruction.

In the simple example shown above, a VM sequence for it might look like this:

```
PUSHQ   [cat dog mouse]
CALL    "length"
CALL    "=>"
```

In practice, as ever, things are more complicated, but the basic principle should be clear. Reference will be made to the virtual machine, and explanations of various POP-11 features will be in terms of their VM code. The VM instructions shown here will be added to in later chapters as the need arises.

PUSHQ   *THING*

Pushes the *THING* onto the user stack. It can be any POP-11 object whatsoever.

POP   *VARIABLENAME*

Pops the top object on the user stack into the named variable. The name of a variable is a POP-11 word.

CALL   *PROCEDURENAME*

Invokes the named procedure. The name of a procedure is a POP-11 word.

Variables in the VM

This POP-11:

```
: vars philosophers;
: [descartes sartre rousseau] -> philosophers;
```

is translated into this VM code:

```
PUSHQ   "philosophers"
CALL    "sysvars"

PUSHQ   [descartes sarte rousseau]
POP     "philosophers"
```

This example shows how variables are made – simply call the procedure for making them. It should be clear that to really understand POP-11, you will need a good knowledge of what procedures there are, what arguments they expect, and what results they produce. As with learning any kind of language, vocabulary is the key to success. Learning the whole POP-11 vocabulary is a daunting task, and is dependent on your implementation, and you would have to consult the documentation which comes with your system. You may find the breadth of the system overwhelming, and lose track of which are important parts to learn about. This book concentrates on a core POP-11 which is sufficient for writing most programs; **sysvars** happens to be a procedure which makes variables, and is not of any real interest.

It is often the case that bits of POP-11 syntax, such as **vars**, translate to VM code which could have been generated in a different way. You may realise that the code generated by the **vars** above could just as easily come from

```
: sysvars("philosophers");
```

Also, where there is special syntax for some common function, like **vars**, the underlying procedure which gets called normally has a different name – in this case **sysvars**.

Values of Variables in the VM

In the politicians example from the previous section, we had this code:

```
: conservative <> labour -> mps;
: mps =>
** [thatcher tebbit fowler kinnock healey livingstone]
```

Here is the original, shown with the VM it generates:

```
: conservative <> labour -> mps;
      PUSHQ   "conservative"
      CALL    "valof"
      PUSHQ   "labour"
      CALL    "valof"
      CALL    "<>"
      POP     "mps"
: mps =>
      PUSHQ   "mps"
      CALL    "valof"
      CALL    "=>"
```

You can see that the two arguments, **conservative** and **labour**, are pushed as words, and then the procedure **valof** is called. In stack terms, **valof** replaces a word on the top of the stack by the value of that word. It takes one argument and produces one result. The argument should be a word which is the name of a variable, and the result will be the value of the variable, that is, the variable which was last put there by the assignment arrow.

As described earlier, <> takes two arguments, and produces a single result, which is a longer list.

An idea which should be clear from examining the VM code in this way is that there is no necessity of putting results into variables. We could simply write:

: conservative <> labour =>
** [thatcher tebbit fowler kinnock healey livingstone]

Also, there is no necessity for objects to be removed from the stack. They can be left on the stack, like this:

: conservative <> labour;

At the end of that instruction, the new list of the six politicians is left sitting on the top of the stack. We can print it out now, like this:

: =>
** [thatcher tebbit fowler kinnock healey livingstone]

Pushing in Real Life

Because getting the value of a variable is such a common action, it should have its own VM instruction. So, instead of following most of the PUSHQs with calls to **valof**, there is normally another VM instruction called PUSH, which pushes the value of a word.

PUSHQ   *THING*

Pushes the *THING* onto the user stack. It can be any POP-11 object whatsoever.

PUSH   *VARIABLENAME*

Pushes the value of the *VARIABLENAME* onto the stack. A variable name is a word. This is exactly the same as

PUSHQ   *VARIABLENAME*
CALL   "valof"

More About the Printarrow

As already shown, the printarrow is the ubiquitous method of printing results. It is very simple to work, and shows the objects in a form so that you can tell what kind of object it is. POP-11 has many procedures for printing objects in different formats, but for simple programs the printarrow is the best method.

So far, all we have seen is the printarrow printing a single object. But you can use the printarrow to print all the objects on the stack. Here is an example where three objects are put onto the stack, and then printed out:

```
: [a]; [b]; [c] =>
** [a] [b] [c]
```

A problem which often confuses newcomers to POP-11 is that they find lots of objects printed out when they were only expecting one. This can happen if you forget to use printarrows, like this:

```
: [a] <> [b];
```

Confusion, because nothing was printed out. So try it again:

```
: [a] <> [b] =>;
** [a b] [a b]
```

And confusion again, because now there are two of them. All that happened was that the first <> made its list normally, and left it on the stack. The second time <> made its list normally, and added it to the stack. The printarrow then printed both of them.

In fact, the printarrow is more complicated than this. Inside procedures, it will print only one object. When it is used at the colon prompt, it prints everything on the stack, another source of confusion for beginners. We will see the printarrow used inside procedures in a later chapter.

More List Procedures

As well as getting at individual elements of a list, it is often useful to get at a pile of them. For example, in the shopping list example, we had

```
: vars shopping;
: [coffee chocolate cream] -> shopping;
: [cocoa ^^ shopping] -> shopping;
: shopping =>
** [cocoa coffee chocolate cream]
```

Another part of the program would have to deal with buying the items, and so they would have to be removed from the list. Suppose we bought the cocoa and the coffee. We could remove them from the list like this:

```
: allbutfirst(2, shopping) -> shopping;
: shopping =>
** [chocolate cream]
```

You should be able to see the relationship between tl and **allbutfirst** – these two examples show it clearly:

```
: tl(shopping) =>
** [cream]
: allbutfirst(1, shopping) =>
** [cream]
```

Not surprisingly, **allbutfirst** has a friend called **allbutlast**. This example should confirm your suspicions:

```
: allbutlast(3, [uno dos tres quatro cinco]) =>
** [uno dos]
```

In the shopping example, we would have a problem if we bought the chocolate first. We had this list:

[cocoa coffee chocolate cream]

and we wanted this:

[cocoa coffee cream]

Of course, it would be possible to use some combination of **allbutfirst**, **allbutlast** and <> to get the right list. However, there is a real problem here. We would have to know where in the list the parts were that we wanted. In general, we won't know this, and we don't (yet) know of a way to find out. POP-11 programs are usually highly symbolic, and have few, if any, numbers in them. What we really want in this example is to write something like this:

: delete("chocolate", shopping) -> shopping;

And we can write exactly this. delete is a procedure for deleting elements of a list, wherever they might be. It actually deletes all the elements which are the same; so if by accident we had added chocolate to the list twice, delete will get rid of both of them. It also doesn't matter if there weren't any instances of chocolate – the list would just be unchanged.

CHAPTER 3

Comparisons, Tests and Matching

Introduction

The last chapter presented some simple ways of manipulating lists and other objects. While they were simple to comprehend, they tend not to be the most useful methods for most programs. This is because most programs work with data which has a relatively rich structure, and need commensurately rich manipulators. This chapter shows methods for comparing POP-11 objects, from the simple to the complex, and for taking them apart and classifying them.

Philosophy

It is not obvious how complex the concept of 'sameness' is – many philosophers have written many words about this very subject, and some of it has relevance here. When writing programs, we often have need to see if two objects are the 'same', and often give the subject too little thought.

The sameness of two objects is entirely dependent on the aspects of the object which are relevant to the purpose in hand. Consider the word 'read', and its relationship with these words:

    red   – same sound
    reed   – same sound as other meaning of 'read'
    dare   – anagram
    read   – same spelling as other meaning of 'read'
    lire   – same meaning but in French

The procedures which POP-11 provides for comparing objects all deal with simple, structure aspects of the objects. It is part of the design of your program to build structures representing the aspects of your data which are important to your program, and then use the built-in features of POP-11 to implement them. As such, most programs require custom-built comparison procedures which compare the features relevant to the specific program.

Comparison Procedures

Almost all of the built-in comparison procedures, and most of those which people write for themselves, return a boolean result. The boolean data type, to recap, covers only two objects; one represents truth, the other falsehood. Programmers familiar

31

with other languages are reminded that these are the only objects used to represent truth and falsehood.

Equality

The simplest comparison you will need is 'equality'. In POP-11, two objects are equal if they are of the same data type, and have equal components. Because this is a commonly used procedure, it is an 'infix operator', and the symbol sits between its arguments, like this:

```
: "hello" = "goodbye" =>
** <false>
```

The English interpretation of this is 'Are these two objects equal?' and the result means 'No'.

The equality test will work on any two objects, and always returns a boolean result. The operation is commutative, which means that if you swap the order of the arguments, the result is the same. (If this seems obvious, consider addition and subtraction.)

The phrase 'have the same structure' used above means, roughly, that the two objects print the same. The following examples should clarify:

A number is never equal to a list, regardless of what the list contains:

```
: 1234 = [1234] =>
** <false>
```

A word is only equal to the same word:

```
: "hello" = "hello" =>
** <true>
```

You have already been advised not to use uppercase letters, as they will make your programs markedly more complex. This is because case is significant in equality comparisons, and POP-11 has no built-in comparisons which ignore case.

```
: "Hello" = "hello" =>
** <false>
```

A list is equal to another list if they both have the same number of elements, and corresponding elements are equal:

```
: [hello mum] = [hello mum] =>
** <true>

: [hello [mum]] = [hello mum] =>
** <false>
```

(Because [mum] is not equal to mum.)

```
: [hello mum] = [[hello mum]] =>
** <false>
```

(Because the first list has two elements, the second has one.)

Comparing numbers is a tricky subject. As mentioned in the section on data types, there are many ways of representing numbers. It is well known that computer arithmetic has some peculiar characteristics, especially because of rounding errors and other implementation problems.

The POP-11 approach to numeric processing has always been that (numerically) naive users will get the results they expect. This is true as long as you stick to relatively straightforward manipulations. 'Equality' for POP-11 numbers, then, means that the two objects represent the same mathematical number. If you are only using numbers to count things, you'll never get into any difficulties. In any case, it is worth reading the documentation of your system to find out what numeric types are supported, and the exact interpretation your system puts on them.

Bearing in mind these caveats, two numbers are equal when they look like they should be:

```
: 41297 = 41297 =>
** <true>
```

As mentioned before, the equality operator can be applied to any two objects, and that includes booleans. There is no special syntax for boolean objects. Instead, there are two variables which contain them, appropriately called true and false. Each of these is only equal to itself:

```
: true = false =>
** <false>

: false = false =>
** <true>
```

Finally, procedures are ordinary data objects just like any other. This is a really useful feature of POP-11, which gives it a tremendous amount of power for some problems. A procedure is only equal to itself:

```
: hd = hd =>
** <true>
```

To summarise, equals (=) is for questions of the form:'Is this object structurally the same as that object.'

Membership

The **delete** procedure was introduced in the last chapter, and was a procedure for deleting elements from lists, where it didn't matter if the object used to be in the list.

In the shopping list example we used, a POP-11 expression like this:

```
: delete("chocolate", shopping) -> shopping;
```

is read as meaning 'Ensure that chocolate is not in the shopping list', while this statement

```
: "chocolate" :: shopping -> shopping;
```

would mean 'Ensure that chocolate is in the shopping list.'

What we now need is to be able to ask 'Is chocolate in the shopping list?' The procedure **member** fits the bill, and would be used like this:

```
: vars shopping;
: [chocolate flour eggs cheese] -> shopping;
: member("flour", shopping) =>
** <true>
: member("milk", shopping) =>
** <false>
```

The first two lines declare a variable, and put a list into it. The intended English interpretation is 'Remember to buy chocolate, flour, eggs and cheese.' Then we find that it is true that flour is on the list, and false that milk is there.

It is clear that **member** must have some rule for deciding whether any item is the same as the candidate you are interested in: it uses the equality described earlier in this chapter.

To summarise, **member** is for questions of the form: 'Is this object in that list?'.

Pattern Matching

The **member** procedure provides a simple method for discovering whether a given object is a member of a given list, and is a very useful procedure. Frequently, however, you will find that it is not powerful enough.

For example, suppose we want to answer the question 'Are there any lists in this list?' or 'Is the second item of this list a word?' Clearly, **member** is not up to questions of this form.

One of the most useful built-in procedures is **matches**, which can express questions like those above, and many more. It is both for asking questions about the structure of lists, and for taking parts out of lists.

As with equals (=), **matches** is an infix procedure, and sits between its arguments. Unlike equals, **matches** cares about the order of its arguments.

The argument on the left is the list you want to ask the question about – we'll call it the candidate.

The argument on the right is a list representing the internal structure you are interested in – we'll call it the pattern.

In the simplest usage, the pattern is just an ordinary list, and **matches** gives the same results as **=**.

```
: [hello mum] matches [hello mum] =>
** <true>

: [hello mum] matches [hello paul] =>
** <false>
```

Matching a Single Unknown Object

Suppose we want to find out if a given list represents a greeting. In our scheme, we'll deem that any list which begins with the word **hello** and then has one more element is a greeting.

Of course, we could use some construction using **hd**, **length** and **=**, but **matches** will give us more flexibility.

The pattern list can contain an equals sign, which means that there must be an element in the candidate list, but it doesn't matter what it is. This use of the equals sign has no relation whatsoever with the use for testing equality.

This fragment of code will test for greetings:

```
: [hello mum] matches [hello =] =>
** <true>
: [hello paul] matches [hello =] =>
** <true>
```

Note that there must be exactly one element which gets matched by the equals sign:

```
: [hello] matches [hello =] =>
** <false>
: [hello mum and paul] matches [hello =] =>
** <false>
```

Finally, note that the object matched by the equals-sign can be any single object, including any single list:

```
: [hello [godzilla kingkong tarzan]] matches [hello =] =>
** <true>
```

To summarise, the single-equals sign in match patterns will match a single object, regardless of what the object is.

Matching Any Number of Unknown Objects

Often, it is useful to match an unknown number of things in a list. Continuing with the previous example, it would probably be more useful if any list which begins with the word hello is considered a greeting.

The double-equals symbol (==) is used in patterns for this: it will match any number of objects in a list. So, to recognise our newly-defined greetings, we can do this:

```
: [hello mum and paul] matches [hello ==] =>
** <true>
```

Here, the == is matched against the last three elements of the candidate list, while the hellos match by the simple equality rule.

The double-equals will match any number of items in the list, including none, as in this example:

```
: [hello] matches [hello ==] =>
** <true>
```

You can use matches like member: here are examples (for the shopping list problem) which will always give the same result:

```
: member("chocolate", shopping) =>
```

and

```
: shopping matches [== chocolate ==] =>
```

The pattern says that there can be any number of items preceding the word chocolate, and followed by any number of items: clearly, this will have the same meaning as the member expression shown above it.

A point about the single-equals and double-equals signs: the double one is formed by two equals characters with nothing in between. So [==] contains one double-equals symbol, while [= =] has two single-equals symbols.

Match patterns can be very complicated, and usually it is a good idea to write down the format of the data in the lists which you will be using. Here are some examples which match relatively complex structures. We'll assume that our candidate list is in a variable called cand.

Will match if cand contains a list:

```
: cand matches [== [==] ==] =>
```

Will match if cand has exactly one element:

```
: cand matches [=] =>
```

Will match if **cand** has more than two items:

  : cand matches [= = ==] =>

Will match if **cand** has the words **beginning, middle** and **ending**, in that order:

  : cand matches [== beginning == middle == ending ==] =>

In the parsetree example of the last chapter, we can make a distinction between 'grammar' subtrees and 'lexical' subtrees. Grammar subtrees, like **nounphrase**, contain other subtrees. Lexical subtrees, like **determiner**, just contain a single word. Here is an example which will match if **cand** is a grammatical subtree (that is, has a list after the first item):

  : cand matches [= == [==] ==] =>

Another parsing example: this will match if **cand** contains a **nounphrase** subtree:

  : cand matches [= == [nounphrase ==] ==] =>

To summarise, the double-equals symbol will match any number of objects in the candidate list, including none.

Exercises

1. Write a pattern which will match
   (a) all three-element lists;
   (b) all three-element lists whose second element is the word **middle**;
   (c) all lists whose second element is the word **second**;
   (d) all lists which begin with **hello** and end with **goodbye**;
   (e) all lists which have the word **interim** between the first and last items;
   (f) all lists which begin with i and contain the word **mother**.

2. Describe in English all the lists which will match these patterns, and write down two examples:
   (a) [== []]
   (b) [[==]]
   (c) [noun =]
   (d) [noun ==]
   (e) [noun dog]

3. Find two lists which don't match any of the patterns in question 2.

4. Find the two lists which match the highest number of the patterns in question 2.

More Matching

The matcher is, as we have seen, a very powerful method for recognising lists of complex description. But, so far, there is no way of finding out exactly which parts of the candidate list matched which parts of the pattern.

Keeping the Unknown Parts

If you want to know what each part of the pattern matched, you use the single- and double-query symbols, in conjunction with variable names. In a pattern, a single-query in front of a variable name will match anything a single-equals will match, and if the match is successful, will put the corresponding object in the variable. Analogously, a double-query in front of a variable name in the pattern will match anything a double-equals will match, and if successful, will put a *list* of the objects from the candidate into the named variable.

Here's a worked example:

Declare some 'match variables' for keeping the components:

    : vars one many;

And make a candidate list:

    : vars cand;
    : [the quick brown fox] -> cand;

Let's see if the candidate ends with fox:

    : cand matches [== fox] =>
    ** <true>

By using ?? in front of a variable name in the pattern list, we can see what the things were in front of fox, like this:

    : cand matches [??many fox] =>
    ** <true>
    : many =>
    ** [the quick brown]

If we just wanted to know what the first element is, we use the single-query, like this:

    : cand matches [?one ==] =>
    ** <true>
    : one =>
    ** the

Of course, you don't have to use the variables as named here; **?** and **??** will work with any variables.

A question which often puzzles newcomers to POP-11 is why the double-query puts a list in the variable, while the single version puts a single item. The answer is simple: the double-query will match any number of items, including none. As they must be parcelled up to be put into one variable, they are collected together as a list. The single query always matches just a single item, and so can simply assign that to the variable.

In summary, in a pattern **?single** will match whatever **=** matches, and **??double** matches whatever **==** matches. In addition, if the match is successful, then the variable named after the **?** or **??** will hold the parts of the candidate list which they were matched against. A single-query always puts a single item in the variable, while the double-query always puts a list of the matched items in the variable.

Some Harder Matching

There are several inherent complexities with a matching procedure such as POP-11's **matches**. This section covers some you might stumble across.

The first is the order of matching. Consider this:

```
: vars left right;
: [so and so] matches [??left so ??right] =>
** <true>
```

It is clear that the candidate does match the list: but how? In this example there are two possibilities:

	left	right
1.	[]	[and so]
2.	[so and]	[]

Both of these are equally 'correct', as they both fit the pattern, which is interpreted as 'any number of items, followed by the word **so**, followed by any number of items.' As there are two instances of the word **so**, there are two solutions to the problem.

Because of the power of the matching procedure, it is easy to find candidates and patterns for which there are a great number of possible solutions. You should not assume that **matches** will find a particular one. We say that the order of matching is undefined. This is especially important because **matches** may be implemented in different ways on different POP-11 systems; and a program which depended on it producing a particular solution when many are possible would probably only work on one system.

A second problem is what happens if a match variable is used more than once in a pattern? Perhaps you might write this:

```
: cand matches [?one == ?one] =>
```

intending it to be a check that the candidate list began and ended with the same item. This is the correct interpretation: a match variable must match the same item in all occurrences of the variable in the pattern. Similarly, double-query match variables must match the same sequence of items in all occurrences. So, to check whether a list consists of two equal halves, it is legitimate to write:

```
: cand matches [??many ??many] =>
```

A possible value for cand where this would match is

[one two three one two three]

A third question concerns the value of match variables if the match fails. Consider this:

```
: vars one;
: [remember me] -> one;
: [hello bonjour ola] matches [?one bonjour elephant] =>
** <false>
```

Clearly this match should fail: but what is the value of the variable one? Some systems would leave it having some value which depended on how far the matching process got (probably hello in this case), while others would leave it completely unchanged by the failed match, holding **[remember me]**. Hopefully POP-11 implementors will choose to standardise on this issue: this author prefers for failed matches to have no side-effects. Until that time, the answer is undefined, and you should not rely on any particular value.

Match Restrictions

Sometimes the basic facilities of matches are not enough, and would match more candidates than is suited to your particular problem. In this case, what is needed is a method to restrict the match.

Suppose you need to find out if a list has any numbers in it. With the tools shown so far, there is no way to do this. First, we need a procedure for recognising numbers, and secondly a method for applying that to lists.

A key concept is the recogniser procedure, also known as a *predicate*. POP-11 has a great number of these built in, and you will probably write some in your programs. Usually, their names are formed from the kind of object recognised, and the word 'is': so in a parsing program, you might find procedures called issentence and isnounphrase and so on.

The recognisers which POP-11 already has are for recognising data types: it has one for each data type, and some others for useful classes of items. A particular one is called **isnumber**, and it takes a single argument, and returns a boolean indicating if it is a number or not:

```
: isnumber([hello]) =>
** <false>
: isnumber("elephant") =>
** <false>
: isnumber(126) =>
** <true>
```

The method for restricting matches is very simple. After a match variable in a pattern, put a colon and the name of a 'restrictor procedure', like this:

```
: vars num;
: cand matches [== num:isnumber ==] =>
```

The pattern here should be read as 'any number of items, followed by a single item which is a number (to be kept in **num**) and followed by any number of items'.

So, if **cand** happened to contain **[socrates is about 2456]**, then after the match, **num** would hold the number **2456**, because the matching of **num** was restricted to numbers.

Fancy Matching

(Can be skipped on first reading.)

In actual programs, the result of the match is less useful than any assignments to match variables that it may do, because when the program is working properly the matches will always succeed.

A good example of this is in a production system, such as might be used in an expert system. Such programs often have data in lists, in a form like this:

```
: vars rulebase;
: [
:   [[complaint is headache] [problems notinclude ulcer]
:     ===>
:     [treatment includes aspirin]
:   ]
:   [[complaint is wound] [severity is minor] [age under 10]
:     ===>
:     [treatment includes kissitbetter]
:     [treatment includes stickyplaster]
:   ]
: ] -> rules;
```

Where the rulebase (in **rules**) is a list of 'productions'. Each production is a list of conditions followed by a list of results, often called 'antecedents' and 'consequents', and separated by some suitable symbol, such as **===>**. For reasons we shall not go into here, we would normally look at each rule in turn, so there might be a stage in the program where there was a variable called **rule** which contained a single rule from the rulebase, and we want to take the rule apart, like this:

```
: rule matches [??ante ===> ??conseq] =>
** <true>
```

Clearly, if the rule didn't match there would be something wrong with the rulebase, because the rule would be ill-formed for this program. But what we really want to do is just get the parts of the rule into the variables **ante** and **conseq**. In a case like this, it is normal to use the 'strict matcher', which comes in the form of an infix operator with the symbol **-->**. The symbol is by analogy with the assignment arrow (**->**), and is formed from two minus signs and a greater-than sign. The strict matcher doesn't produce a result, so we just follow it with a semicolon:

```
: rule --> [??ante ===> ??conseq];
```

The real point about the strict matcher is that if the match fails, it produces a mishap message – which is surely appropriate, as it indicates an error with the program. The message would be 'Non-matching arguments for -->'.

To summarise, **-->** is just like **matches**, except that no result is returned, and where **matches** would have failed, **-->** produces a mishap.

In some advanced uses of **matches**, the patterns become very complicated indeed, and the programming around them is too intricate to be clear. To help with such cases, POP-11 provides **matchesoneof** and **matchesallof**. These are both infix procedures, like **matches**, but the right hand argument is a list of patterns, not a pattern itself. As can be inferred from the names, with **matchesoneof**, the candidate list must match at least one of patterns in the patterns list; and with **matchesallof** it must match all of the patterns in the patterns list.

There is an added bonus with **matchesallof**, and that is that any match variables must match the same things wherever they occur in the list of patterns.

CHAPTER 4

Procedure Definition

Up to this stage, POP-11 has been presented in terms of its data structures and a few of the more useful built-in procedures. These will comprise your basic box of tools for building programs with. They have been presented as simple incantations to be tried at the terminal, with the printarrow to see the results. What is needed now is some method for putting procedural structure around them.

POP-11 provides a number of mechanisms for defining procedures of various types. By far the most common of these is the simple, common-or-garden procedure. First, we'll show a simple definition, and then before going deeply into the mechanics of procedure definition, a few semantic issues need clarifying, to do with variables and results.

A Simple Procedure Definition

A good approach to programming involves separating the primitive data types from the objects they are to represent. We have used a shopping list example before, and it is illustrative here.

As shown previously, we can add items to a list using the cons procedure (::). However, this is a built-in operation which works on lists. What we want for our program are operations which work on shopping requirements.

Here is the definition for the procedure **want**, which we will use when we want to buy another item.

```
define want(item, wanted) -> newwanted;
vars item wanted newwanted;
    item :: wanted -> newwanted;
enddefine;
```

Hopefully the intent of this procedure will be clear: it takes the new thing we want, the current list of wanted things, and builds a new list of wanted things with the :: construction on its third line.

First, some terminology: **want** is the procedure's name; **item**, **wanted**, and **newwanted** are 'local variables'; of these, **item** and **wanted** are 'input variables', and **newwanted** is an 'output variable', or 'result variable'. (Input variables are sometimes known as 'formal parameters' or 'formal arguments'.)

The inputs to a procedure are the things we want it to work on; input variables are

43

places to keep those things. Outputs are the product of the work; output variables are places to keep them. Applied to

```
: 2 + 3 =>
** 5
```

The inputs were 2 and 3, and the result was 5.

For the English interpretation of defining, consider what we are trying to do. After we have succeeded in defining our procedure, we should be able to call it like any other procedure, like this:

want("chocolate", shopping) -> shopping;

Because we have no idea what actual variables or objects we will call the procedure with, we have to substitute **want**'s internal names for them. In this case, we have called the first argument **item**, the second **wanted** and the result is **newwanted**. So, for the purposes of naming these things within the procedure, we have transformed our invocation above into

want(item, wanted) -> newwanted;

Now, we couldn't just make do with this as the definition, because it is syntactically identical to a call of the procedure: instead, we stick **define** in front of it, to say that we are defining the meaning of the expression. You should read

define *SOMETHING*;
    METHOD
enddefine;

as being a definition for statements of the form that *SOMETHING* is in, and where POP-11 sees a statement of that form, it does the *METHOD* in the body of the procedure. In the example above, the *SOMETHING* was

want(item, wanted) -> newwanted;

As an example of what would 'have the same form', we could have

want([isabard kingdom brunel], []) =>

or

want(6, nicenumbers) -> numbers;

All that matters is that the procedure has a result, and that it takes two arguments. (In actual fact, there are many ways to invoke procedures in POP-11, and all of those will be defined too. But this is the canonical form of the call to **want**: with the right number of arguments between the parentheses, and with a result being printed or assigned to a variable.)

Global and Local Variables – Syntax

Before this chapter, all you will have seen are global variables. These are so called because they are accessible from all parts of all programs: the 'whole world'. Now, with procedure definitions, you are presented with local variables, so called because they are only accessible from a locality. It does not make sense for a variable to be local except with reference to a procedure that it is local to.

What is the difference? Syntactically, a global variable is declared outside of procedures, and locals are declared inside them. An example:

```
vars world;

define foo( );
vars town;
enddefine;
```

Here, world is a global variable, because it is declared outside of all procedures. And town is a local because it is declared within the define ... enddefine of foo.

The next question is about the scope of the variables: where can they be accessed from. Actually, in POP-11, the full answer is not so simple to explain. POP-11 has what is known as 'dynamic scoping', which means the accessibility of variables is dependent on how the program runs. For the present purposes, we will say that local variables are only accessible from within the procedure they are declared in, and global variables are accessible from all procedures, and outside of procedures.

Here's an example:

```
: vars world;
: define foo( );
: vars town;
:     [local] -> town;
:     [global] -> world;
: enddefine;
```

So, at this point, all the variables are uninitialised. It is legal to refer to world inside the procedure foo because world is a global. So, check the values of them:

```
: world =>
** <undef world>
: town =>
** <undef town>
```

And as you should have expected, both are undef objects. Now, run foo, and see what effect this has on the variables:

```
: foo( );
: world =>
** [global]
: town =>
** <undef town>
```

As you can see, world has been changed, but town has not. This is because foo has its own private, local, copy of town which was changed. But that disappeared as soon as foo finished.

Local Variables – Semantics

There is no straightforward story which makes dynamic scoping rules easier to understand. The best way is the truth.

A variable actually exists in only a single place. All references to the variable refer to the same place. But when a variable is a local of a procedure, that procedure saves its previous value somewhere safe as soon as the procedure starts. Then the procedure does its work, and afterwards, the very last thing it does is to restore the local variable from the safe place. Programmers familiar with LISP and assembler code should recognise this mechanism: programmers used to other languages might find it difficult.

So, instead of talking about global and local variables, we should really talk about global and local *values* of variables. A consequence of this is that at different points in your program, the same variable refers to different values. Another consequence is that from a procedure's point of view, all values of variables are either local to the procedure, or global to it. Its variables simply inherit a value; it is quite possible that that value was given to it locally by some other procedure.

You should take the time to work through and understand the following example, to see where each value of the variable x is saved and restored.

```
vars x;
define goo( );
vars x;
    [goo one ^x] =>
    "mango" -> x;
    [goo two ^x] =>
enddefine;
define foo( );
vars x;
    [foo one ^x] =>
    "pomegranate" -> x;
    goo( );
    [foo two ^x] =>
enddefine;
```

If we run these procedures like this:

```
: "ox" -> x;
: foo();
: x =>
```

What gets printed out? Remembering that the variable **x** is local to both procedures, (and referring to the previous chapter on list manipulations for the messages) . . .

At **vars x;** the variable is created, and so it has its value set to the undef object <**undef x**>. Then we put the word **ox** into it. Then we call **foo**. The first thing **foo** does is save the values of its locals: in this case just **x**. So, **foo** has squirrelled away the value **ox**. Then **foo** prints a message out, and so you would see

   ** [foo one ox]

Then **foo** assigns the word **pomegranate** to **x**. Then it calls **goo**. As you will see, **x** is a local here too. So **goo** squirrels away the value **pomegranate**. Then it prints its first message, and we see:

   ** [goo one pomegranate]

Then **goo** assigns the word **mango** to **x**, and prints out its second message:

   ** [goo two mango]

So much for **goo**: the last thing it does is restore **x**'s previous value which it had kept: **pomegranate**. Then it returns to its caller, in this case **foo**. Looking back at **foo**, you will see that it prints another message too:

   ** [foo two pomegranate]

And that was **foo**'s swansong: its last task is to restore its local **x** to its saved value **[global]**. And after the call we had made to **foo**, we print **x** for ourselves: we see

   ** ox

Local Variables – In Practice

You may find the description above on dynamic scoping difficult. In normal usage, local variables are extremely straightforward. It is only when things go wrong with your program, or in some intricate programming, that you will need to apply the full truth.

In normal use, making a variable local to a procedure just means that the procedure wants a private variable to do what it likes with, which won't cause problems to other procedures. You will see that the majority of variables are local, because if you mostly use global variables, you will inevitably forget which procedures use which, and get bugs in your programs. Languages such as BASIC have only global variables: it is one of several weaknesses which make that language cripplingly difficult to write large programs in. A typical large POP-11 program might have half a dozen global variables; but several hundred locals.

Incidentally, it makes no difference where you declare variables within a procedure: they will all act as though they had been declared at the beginning, which is the conventional place to put the **vars** statement. Also, any input and output variables are automatically local to the procedure. You may still like to put them in the **vars** statement, just to remind yourself that they are local.

Exercises A

1. Assuming you have a clean slate, as when you first enter POP-11, and you try the following things, what is printed? Try these questions first without the machine; use it for help if you need to.

```
: vars dog;

: define one();
:     [uno] -> dog;
: enddefine;

: define two();
: vars dog;
:     [dos] -> dog;
: enddefine;

: define three();
:     one();
: enddefine;

: define four();
:     two();
: enddefine;

: define five(dog);
:     one();
: enddefine;
```

(a) : dog =>
(b) : one(); dog =>
(c) : [] -> dog; two(); dog =>
(d) : [] -> dog; three(); dog =>
(e) : [] -> dog; four(); dog =>
(f) : [] -> dog; five(); dog =>

2. Same as question 1: what gets printed? If you can do this question, you'll never have any trouble.

```
: vars cat;
: define show();
:     cat =>
: enddefine;

: define ein()
:     show();
:     [kitty] -> cat;
: enddefine;

: define zwei();
:     ein();
:     show();
: enddefine;

: define drei();
:     zwei();
:     show();
: enddefine;

: define vier();
: vars cat;
:     [katze] -> cat;
:     drei();
:     show();
: enddefine;

: vier();
: show();
```

Local Variables, Arguments and Results – Virtual Machine

The clearest way of understanding arguments and results of procedures is by way of the virtual machine. This section explains both of these, along with the local variable mechanism, in terms of VM instructions, the theoretical basis of POP-11.

Procedures, both built-in and those you define, can have any number of arguments, including none, and any number of results. Normally, procedures take a fixed number of arguments and results, and although it is possible to vary both, having a variable number of arguments is unusual and messy.

There may be implementation restrictions on the number of arguments. Typically, procedures may be limited to several hundred arguments; and the number of results is limited only by memory. Neither of these should cause any problems.

In practice, procedures will only have a few arguments: ten would be very unusual. Procedures can be classified into three groups by the number of results they have: zero, one, or many.

As presented earlier, all arguments and results go through an 'open' stack. Passing the arguments to a procedure merely involves stacking them. Results are removed either by a procedure taking its arguments, or by assigning them into variables. Remember that this is true of every procedure, including built-in ones such as **+**.

Because all items on the stack are created equal, there isn't really any distinction between 'arguments' and 'results': instead there are simply objects on the stack. The difference is in the mind of the programmer: something is an argument if it is removed by a procedure taking its arguments; something is a result if it is put there by a procedure. Clearly the same object can be the result of one procedure and the argument to another: the difference lies in whether you are interested in its origin or its destiny.

To show how the local variables work, we need some more VM instructions, for implementing the squirrelling and restoring functions described in the section above on local variables.

SAVE   <variable name>, <variable name>...

Saves the values of the named variables in a safe place, which is private to the current procedure. The variable names are words.

RESTORE   <variable name>, <variable name>...

Restores the values of the named variables from the safe place which is private to the current procedure. The variable names are words, and must have been saved before.

So, what VM instructions do we need to express our simple procedure? Here it is again:

```
define want(item, wanted) -> newwanted;
vars item wanted newwanted;
    item :: wanted -> newwanted;
enddefine;
```

And this is the VM code for it. First, we have to squirrel away the local variables:

```
SAVE        "item", "wanted", "newwanted"
```

Then get our arguments: notice these are done 'backwards' (right to left), because things get reversed on the stack.

```
POP         "wanted"
POP         "item"
```

Then we have to do the body of the procedure. In this case, it is a simple call to another procedure, and keeping the result. We push the arguments 'forwards' (left to right):

```
PUSH        "item"
PUSH        "wanted"
CALL        "::"
POP         "newwanted"
```

That's the bulk of this procedure done. But we have to push the result of the procedure, which is in the variable **newwanted**:

```
PUSH        "newwanted"
```

Now we just clean up the local variables, and that's it.

```
RESTORE     "item", "wanted", "newwanted"
```

If you look at the VM code all together, you may realise that there are other ways of writing POP-11 which give rise to procedures which behave exactly the same. The issue here is not efficiency, but programming style. Efficiency in matters like this is usually more than taken care of by compiler optimisations. Here's the code all together, with the lines numbered:

```
1    SAVE        "item", "wanted", "newwanted"
2    POP         "wanted"
3    POP         "item"
4    PUSH        "item"
5    PUSH        "wanted"
6    CALL        "::"
7    POP         "newwanted"
8    PUSH        "newwanted"
9    RESTORE     "item", "wanted", "newwanted"
```

Notice the POP–PUSH on lines 7 and 8: after the call to cons, we pop a result into the local variable **newwanted**. Because it is the result variable, it then gets pushed again immediately as this is the end of the procedure. A lot of people write this kind of procedure in a different way, with an implicit stacking of the result, like this:

```
define want(item, wanted);
    item :: wanted;
enddefine;
```

As a matter of programming style, the first method is probably better, because you can see clearly that **want** is intended to have a result, and that its author believed (correctly) that :: has a result. On general principles, it is a good thing if procedures can be examined on their own, without reference to other procedures, and be seen to be correct. An English interpretation of the first style is that **item** is consed onto **wanted** which produces a result, which is (locally) called **newwanted**, which is the result of the procedure. The second one says that the results, if any, of the consing are going to be the results of **want**. So if you need to know if there are results of **want**, you have to find out the results of cons. Of course, with a common built-in procedure such as cons, the answer will be well-known. However, the principle comes more into play when the called procedures are your own; or even more so when they are written by someone else.

The second style is shown here, and used in this book, because it is a common idiom, especially for such short procedures as this.

To summarise:

Local Variables: The values are saved at the beginning of a procedure, and restored at the end. This way, anything this procedure does to them will be private to itself.

Argument Variables: These are popped from the stack into local variables, remembering that the rightmost argument variable wants the most-recently pushed object.

Result Variables: These are pushed onto the stack from a local variable.

Procedure Calls: Simply push all the things between the parentheses (or both sides of an operator), and then call the procedure.

Exercise B

1. What is the VM code for the shorter version of **want**?

Notice that the list of local variables is shorter, and that the definition of **want** says that the result of **want** is whatever is the result of the call to ::.

Procedure Definition – Experiments

This section describes some experiments you should try on your system, to get used to defining small procedures. You are recommended to use an editor of some kind, unless you are a very accurate typist. Editors on POP-11 systems vary greatly, and you will have to use the documentation which comes with your system in order to find out how to use it. It is probable that you can run pieces of code within the editor – this is the POP-11 way of doing things.

As most of the tools presented in this book are to do with list processing, you should try your hand at writing some small list manipulating procedures. Here's one which doubles a list:

```
define double(list) -> result;
    list <> list -> result;
enddefine;
```

Exercises C

1. Write some procedures, and try them:

(a) A procedure which takes an arbitrary object, and a list, and returns a longer list whose last object is the argument. It should begin like this:

define addback(obj, list) -> newlist;

and should work like this:

: addback("guards", [engine coal passenger post]) =>
** [engine coal passenger post guards]

(b) A procedure which takes an arbitrary object and a list, and adds the object to both ends of the list.

Begins:

define addboth(item, list) -> pushmepullu;

Works:

: addboth("face", [legs body legs]) =>
** [face legs body legs face]

(c) Write a procedure which takes an arbitrary object and a list, and returns a list with the object at the front and nowhere else in the list. This kind of procedure is quite commonly used to implement sets in POP-11, out of lists. (A set is a unordered collection of objects without duplications.) Tip: remember delete.

Works like this:

: setadd("horse", [dog cat]) =>
** [horse dog cat]
: setadd("mouse", [dog cat mouse donkey]) =>
** [mouse dog cat donkey]

(d) A procedure which works like this:

: double([hello there]) =>
** [hello there hello there]

(e) A procedure which works like this:

: twin([hello there]) =>
** [[hello there] [hello there]]

(f) A procedure which starts like this:

define setremove(element, set) -> newset;

(g) A procedure which works like this:

```
: addlen([]) =>
** [0]
: addlen([hello there]) =>
** [2 hello there]
```

2. What do these procedures do? Try them on your system to make sure.

   (a) ```
       define embed(thing) -> result;
           [^thing] -> result;
       enddefine;
       ```

   (b) ```
       define nounphrase(det, noun) -> np;
           [nounphrase ^det ^noun] -> np;
       enddefine;
       ```

   (c) ```
       define isnounphrase(np) -> result;
           np matches [nounphrase [==] [==]] -> result;
       enddefine;
       ```

   (d) ```
       define nodogs1(list) -> newlist;
           delete("dog", list) -> newlist;
       enddefine;
       ```

   (e) ```
       define nodogs2(animals);
           delete("dog", animals);
       enddefine;
       ```

   (f) ```
       define nodogs3(animals);
           delete("dog", animals) =>
       enddefine;
       ```

The Shopping List for the Last Time

How would the simple shopping list be done, properly, in POP-11? Here it is in procedural form, followed by some observations.

```
;;; a global variable for the shopping list itself
;;;
vars shopping;

;;; a procedure for adding things to the list
;;;
define want(item);
    item :: delete(item, shopping) -> shopping;
enddefine;
```

```
;;; a procedure for removing things when we no
;;; longer want them
;;;
define forget(item);
    delete(item, shopping) -> shopping;
enddefine;

;;; and one for buying things
;;;
define bought(item);
    delete(item, shopping) -> shopping;
enddefine;

;;; initialisation
;;;
define setup();
    [] -> shopping;
enddefine;
```

Notice the three actions: adding things to the list, deciding we no longer want something, and buying things. And why do we need a **setup** procedure? What happens if you don't run it?

You'll notice that the procedures **forget** and **bought** have exactly the same effect: there are two procedures because probably, at some time in the future, someone would expand this program by adding a global variable **larder**, and adding a procedure **eat**. Then, **bought** would not only remove things from **shopping**, but add them to **larder**. The procedure **eat** would remove things from the larder. You might want to try expanding this program in that way. Perhaps add a list for items in the shop, and a procedure for buying them. What should your program do if we can't buy things because they aren't in the shop?

CHAPTER 5

Conditions, Loops and Conjunctions

Every programming language provides methods for testing conditions and performing different actions depending on the results. POP-11 is no exception. There are several constructions which suit different circumstances, and which are closely related. In order to make full use of them, you must have a clear understanding of how POP-11 evaluates boolean expressions, and how it takes decisions depending on results.

This chapter presents the many looping and testing contructs in POP-11, and at the end shows how procedures can return without getting to the **enddefine**.

The Simple Condition

The simplest form of conditional expression just means 'if such-and-such is the case, do these actions'. In POP-11, you use the keyword **if**, followed by the 'such-and-such', followed by the keyword **then**, followed by the 'actions', all finished off with the keyword **endif**.

Here is a simple procedure which has a conditional expression in it:

```
define dogcheck(animals);
    if member("dog", animals) then
        [got a dog] =>
    endif;
enddefine;
```

This procedure should be very simple to understand. It takes one argument, which is assumed to be a list. Then it uses **member** to find out if the word **dog** is one of the list's elements; if it is, we get a message printed. If it isn't, nothing happens. (The argument is assumed to be a list because **member** will cause a mishap if its second argument isn't a list.)

```
: dogcheck([cat dog bat weasel]);
** [got a dog]

: dogcheck([cat rat bat]);

: dogcheck([dog]);
** [got a dog]
```

56

The first example call was with a list with dog in it, so our dogcheck procedure printed the message. The second wasn't, so you see no message; and of course [dog] has a dog in it.

Conditionals with else Clauses

Clearly, you might want to do two different things depending on the result of a test, or you might want to do an action unless some condition were the case. POP-11 copes with both of these.

The if construction allows a lot of variations. Here's a procedure which has an else-clause:

```
define dogcheck2(animals);
    if member("dog", animals) then
        [got a dog] =>
    else
        [no dogs here] =>
    endif;
enddefine;
```

Equally, this procedure should make sense as it stands: all the stuff between the then and the else gets done if the condition is true; all the stuff between the else and the endif gets done otherwise.

If you want an action when some condition isn't the case, you could write it using if ... then else ... endif; and put your actions in the else section, and put nothing between then and else. This works fine, but your procedure would look ugly. Instead, you can use the unless construction:

```
define dogcheck3(animals);
    unless member("dog", animals) then
        [dogfree zone] =>
    endunless;
enddefine;
```

The unless statement means 'unless dog is an element of animals, print the message [dogfree zone]'. Some people find unless statements very difficult to use, even though they understand the concepts perfectly well. Here's an example, similar to one presented in the chapter on list manipulations, which might help if you have this problem.

Suppose we want to maintain a list of things, but don't want duplications in it. This is a procedure to add an item to a list *unless* it is already there:

```
define additem(item, list) -> list;
    unless member(item, list) then
        item :: list -> list;
    endunless;
enddefine;
```

(A note about the **define** line: this declares the procedure to have two arguments, the first to be called item, the second list. It also says that the procedure returns a result, which is the value of the variable list. So, whatever the value of list is by the end of the procedure, that will be the result of the procedure.)

Syntactic Aspects of Conditionals

The procedures shown so far have had only one action to be done depending on the condition: this has been for simplicity only. You can put any amount of stuff in the appropriate places. Here's a verbose rewriting of **dogcheck2**:

```
define dogcheck2verbose(animals);
    if member("dog", animals) then
        [got a dog] =>
        [whoopie there is a dog here] =>
        [and it was in this list ^animals] =>
    else
        [no dogs here] =>
        [sniff sniff] =>
        [perhaps we should add one to ^animals] =>
    endif;
enddefine;
```

Of course, you can put any POP-11 code in the action sections of conditionals: including other conditionals. Some programmers of other languages consider nested conditionals to be very bad style; most POP-11 programmers would never be without them.

You can also put any POP-11 code which leaves a result on the stack in the condition sections of conditionals. So far, the examples have just used incantations of **member**, but you could have quite complicated expressions, which are detailed later. Just one example:

```
if hd(animals) = "dog" then
    ...
```

The keyword-endkeyword structure of POP-11 is rigorous throughout: all 'opening' keywords such as **define** and **if** have matching 'closing' keywords **enddefine**, **endif** and so on.

Notice the indentation of the example procedures. While the exact style of indentation is a matter for personal taste, you should get used to indenting your procedures to make them easier to read. This becomes obvious when you start writing procedures with nested conditions, as the structure of the code becomes completely opaque without it. The style used in this book is one of several popular ones; indent after each opening keyword such as if, and put middle keywords such as then on the same line as the opener. Use tabs for indentation, rather than spaces, as it is much easier to keep things lined up. Mostly, POP-11 is indented with four spaces per tab, rather than the more conventional eight, as this takes up less space. You will probably find that your editor will have some method of helping with the indentation.

Conditionals with elseif Clauses

A further feature of if statements is the elseif clause. The best example in English for its intent is a child asking for ice cream: 'I want chocolate, but if I can't have that I want strawberry, and if I can't have that I want vanilla." This kind of expression has uses other than for ice cream, but here is the program for the child:

```
define chooseice(inshop) -> chosen;
    if member("chocolate", inshop) then
        "chocolate" -> chosen;
    elseif member("strawberry", inshop) then
        "strawberry" -> chosen;
    elseif member("vanilla", inshop) then
        "vanilla" -> chosen;
    else
        "apologies" -> chosen;
    endif;
enddefine;
```

In a if statement with elseif clauses, evaluation proceeds like this: try the condition for the if, and if successful, do the actions for it, then skip to past the endif. If unsuccessful, try the condition for the first elseif, and if that is successful, do its actions and then past the endif. Then the remaining elseif clauses are done in the same way. If the last elseif condition fails, do the actions for the else, if present.

You use the multiple conditional test to express the order in which the conditions are tested, and can have as many elseif clauses as you like. Then you can have an else clause, if appropriate.

You could write this procedure without the elseif clauses, but it wouldn't be as easy to understand. If you are uncomfortable with them, practise them. As an illustration, chooseice could be rewritten in the following way, which would be considered poor POP-11 style:

```
define uglychooseice(inshop) -> chosen;
    if member("chocolate", inshop) then
        "chocolate" -> chosen;
    else if member("strawberry", inshop) then
            "strawberry" -> chosen;
        else if member("vanilla", inshop) then
                "vanilla" -> chosen;
            else
                "apologies" -> chosen;
            endif;
        endif;
    endif;
enddefine;
```

A word about **else** clauses: it is considered vital programming style to have **else** clauses when some action must have been performed by the end of the **if** statement (ie, at the **endif**). In the ice cream example, the **else** statement was necessary because the procedure returned a result, and so the program must return a sensible result. Many programs have floundered because their authors *assumed* that one of the **if** or **elseif** clauses would succeed. In tests where the whole point is that some action must happen or must not happen, **else** clauses are redundant: as in the **additem** procedure above.

A word about the **apologies** offered as the result of no wanted ice cream: this is not conventional POP-11 style. Really, the procedure should return some other data type to indicate no ice cream. The assumed convention in the **chooseice** procedure is that words indicate flavour; some other data type should be used to indicate absence. Conventional POP-11 style would return the boolean object <**false**> here, for reasons shown later in this chapter. After all, the child would not suffer apologies as a flavour of ice cream.

How the Testing Works

The descriptions of the conditions being tested by **if** and **unless** have carefully avoided the phrases 'is true' and 'is false', even though this is the normal terminology for them. Instead, we say that an **if** clause will do its actions if its condition is 'successful'. POP-11 uses a simple scheme for defining 'successful', both for efficiency and parsimony, but describing it is a little intricate.

A short example procedure for reference:

```
define explain(object);
    if object then
        [something else section] =>
    else
        [false section] =>
    endif;
enddefine;
```

When testing an object for the purposes of a conditional expression, POP-11 compares it against the boolean object <false>.

So, in the explain procedure, if object is <false>, it will print [false section]. If the object *wasn't* <false>, it will do the other section. In other words, the condition is deemed successful if it doesn't evaluate to <false>, and unsuccessful if it does.

If you are uncertain about this, try defining explain on your system, and try these examples and others of your own:

```
: explain(false);
** [false section]
```

```
: explain(true);
** [something else section]
```

```
: explain([a silly list]);
** [something else section]
```

This final example illustrates the point: any POP-11 object which isn't <false> will make the if succeed. The obvious object which fits the bill is <true>: but lists, numbers and all the other things also work.

The reason for this is twofold. The first is that for procedures which return a computed result, we can return an object which indicates failure in that computation. You will see examples of this later – and a mightily useful technique it is too. Secondly, it makes things go faster, and makes implementation much simpler. An interesting exercise is to consider the implications of testing every condition against both <true> and <false>.

You should be warned that when POP-11 programmers describe a condition as having been 'true', it doesn't mean that it evaluated to <true> – they normally mean that it didn't evaluate to <false>.

Mixing if and unless

There are some variants on the basic conditional which most programmers don't use: you may choose to skip this section and stay with the majority.

As you might appreciate, if and unless are isomorphic; so if elseif makes sense, so does elseunless, and POP-11 has it. Also, if else makes sense with if, it will make sense with unless. Furthermore, whether you start the conditional with if or unless, you can put in elseif *or* elseunless clauses.

To illustrate this usage, the following three procedures behave exactly the same. They have been written to be grotesque: if you can cope with these, you'll never have any trouble in a real programming situation.

```
define samel(a);
    if a = [one] then
        1 =>
    elseif a = [two] then
        2 =>
    else
        3 =>
    endif;
enddefine;

define same2(a);
    unless a /= [one] then
        1 =>
    endunless a /= [two] then
        2 =>
    else
        3 =>
    endunless;
enddefine;

define same3(a);
    if a = [one] then
        1 =>
    elseunless a /= [two] then
        2 =>
    else
        3 =>
    endif;
enddefine;
```

Exercises A

The example programs in these sections have printed things out. Usually, procedures return results: as they will in these questions. Part of learning to program involves learning how to give procedures and variables sensible, systematic names. Part of learning a language involves making sense of it purely from the structures. The procedures have been easy to understand because the names of variables gave clues as to their intended operation. In these questions, some of the names are abstract, to concentrate on the structure.

1. Consider this procedure:

```
define q1(a, b, list) -> res;
    if member(a, list) then
        if member(b, list) then
            [^a ^b] -> res;
        else
            [^a] -> res;
        endif;
    elseif member(b, list) then
        [^b] -> res;
    else
        false -> res;
    endif;
enddefine;
```

What do these invocations print?

(a) : q1(2, 3, [1 2 3]) =>
(b) : q1(2, 3, [3 2 1]) =>
(c) : q1(2, 3, [elephant surprise]) =>
(d) : q1(2, 3, [[2] 3 1]) =>
(e) : q1("cat", "dog", [what a small cat]) =>
(f) : q1([2], [3], [[2] 3 1]) =>

2. A very similar procedure to the previous one:

```
define q2(xx, yy, zz) -> aa;
    [] -> aa;
    if member(yy, zz) then
        yy :: aa -> aa;
    endif;
    if member(xx, zz) then
        xx :: aa -> aa;
    endif;
enddefine;
```

If you try all the example calls of the previous question on q2, which answers come out different?

3. Write a procedure q3 by adding another if statement just before the **enddefine** of q2, so that q3 always gives the same results as q1. What do you need to add?

4. How many calls to **member** are made for each of the calls to q1 and friends? Are they the same for q1, q2, and q3? Write down what **member's** arguments and results are for the call in question 1 (f).

5. Which of q1, q2 and q3 do you think is the best? Why?

6. Write a procedure which returns **[espresso]** if you give it the list **[small black coffee]**. It should begin:

  define italianfor(english) -> italian;

7. Extend **italianfor** so that it knows that **[cappuccino]** is a large white coffee.

8. Does your translation program do something sensible when you go beyond its vocabulary?

More Expressions: Boolean Operators

A common need is to test for several things as a time, as expressed in English like this: 'Don't drink and drive.' These operations, the subject of much study by logicians, are easily expressed in POP-11, like this:

```
define badperson(person, drunks, drivers);
    if member(person, drunks) and
            member(person, drivers) then
        true;
    else
        false;
    endif;
enddefine;
```

This procedure would be used like this:

```
: badperson("pooh", [piglet tigger], [pooh tigger]) =>
** <false>

: badperson("tigger", [piglet tigger], [pooh tigger]) =>
** <true>
```

It has the obvious interpretation: **and** takes two arguments, and if they are both non-<false> then the answer is <true>, otherwise it is <false>.
Similarly, **or** returns <true> if at least one of its arguments isn't <false>.
These functions are commonly defined by 'truth tables', which look like this:

Arguments		Results	
left	right	and	or
T	T	\<true\>	\<true\>
T	\<false\>	\<false\>	\<true\>
\<false\>	T	\<false\>	\<true\>
\<false\>	\<false\>	\<false\>	\<false\>

Note: T here represents any non-\<false\> object.

Some important points to note about these two: and and or are not ordinary procedures, they are keywords. And as such, they have a special property that saves them some work. In common with all of POP-11, evaluation is defined to be left to right, but these two operations don't bother with arguments which can't affect the result. So if the expression on the left of an and is \<false\>, it doesn't bother doing the expression on the right. So in the example above to see if Pooh bear is a bad person (as if it were likely), there is no call to see if pooh is a member of the list drivers.

In fact, the POP-11 boolean operators have a further subtlety in the result which they return. In the table above, and and or are shown as returning a boolean result, and you can think of them doing this if you like. But because the conditionals only ever test against \<false\>, the boolean operators actually can return any non-\<false\> object to indicate truth. So, and will actually return its second (rightmost) argument where T is shown in the table. The or operator will actually return its first non-\<false\> argument where T is shown in the table. Some examples:

```
: true and 1 =>
** 1

: false or [] =>
** []

: [hello] or [] =>
** [hello]
```

POP-11 has another boolean function: not. This is an ordinary procedure, and is often used with and and or. It takes a single argument, and returns the logical opposite, as defined by this truth table:

Argument	not
T	<false>
<false>	<true>

Note: T here represents any non-<false> object.

A Loop For Every Occasion

POP-11 has an impressive array of constructs for performing a sequence of actions several times. They are suited to different applications, and some of them share the same opening keyword, but vary in the middle. It is possible to classify them according to what kind of purpose they serve:

Conditional Loops
>   For when a condition (result of a procedure, value of a variable) says when to loop or not to loop.   (while, until)

Repetitive and Infinite Loops
>   For when you want your actions executed a particular number of times, or indefinitely.   (repeat)

Structural Loops
>   For when you want to inspect each element of a list.   (for)

Numeric Loops
>   For when you want to execute your actions with a particular variable holding a different number each time.   (for)

General Points

In general, a loop contains a body and a condition. The condition is checked each time the code in the body is executed, and decides when to stop looping. In POP-11, all the built-in looping constructs test the condition first, and only if appropriate, then execute the body. So the code in the body may never get executed. Programmers used to loops which test 'at the bottom' should take especial note.

Conditional Loops

In harmony with **if** and **unless** are two looping constructs, which perform a test and some actions each time round the loop. There are two forms: **while**, analogous to **if**; and **until**, analogous to **unless**.

The syntax for **while** and **until** is essentially the same: opening keyword; the test expression; the keyword **do**; the actions, and a closing keyword. And their uses are very similar.

Here's a simple example procedure that makes a list which is the same length as the argument list, but with different elements:

```
define makelist(list) -> result;
    [] -> result;
    until length(result) = length(list) do
        "hello" :: result -> result;
    enduntil;
enddefine;
```

The things to note about **while** and **until** are that the test is done first, and then the actions if appropriate, and then the test again, and so on, until the test fails. A consequence of this is that the actions may not ever get executed: in the example above, the action won't get executed if the argument list is the empty list.

With **until**, the test *fails* if it returns <false>. With **while**, test *succeeds* if it returns <false>.

The places where **while** and **until** are the best choice are fairly obscure: it is best just to keep them in mind until your programming demands them.

Repetitive Loops

If you need some actions performed a certain number of times, you need the **repeat** construct, which is perhaps the simplest of all the looping constructs. It consists of the keyword **repeat**, an expression which evaluates to a number, the keyword **times**, then the actions to be performed, and then the closing keyword **endrepeat**.

This procedure makes a list of hellos of a given length:

```
define manyhellos (count) -> result;
    [] -> result;
    repeat count times
        "hello" :: result -> result;
    endrepeat;
enddefine;
```

Extraordinarily simple. In common with all POP-11 looping constructs, the body may not get executed at all. In this procedure, that would happen if the argument count was given as zero. If the expression doesn't evaluate to a number, or is negative, you will get a mishap.

There is another variant of **repeat**, which at present won't look very useful: the endless loop. It consists of the keywords **repeat forever**, then the actions, then **endrepeat**. Here's a very silly program, which prints [hello] forever:

```
define silly();
    repeat forever
        [hello] =>
    endrepeat;
enddefine;
```

This construct would only be useful if there were some way of breaking out of the loop in midstream: which there is. It is called **return**, and is presented later.

Structural Loops

Perhaps the most common operation performed on lists is doing some operation on each of their elements in turn. As it really is so useful, there is a special syntax for this, which uses the keyword **for**. There are several kinds of loop which use this keyword; they have various 'middling' keywords which differentiate them syntactically. Semantically, they are quite distinct.

The structural loop consists of the keyword **for**, then a variable name, the keyword **in**, then an expression which evaluates to a list, the keyword **do**, the actions, and the closing keyword **endfor**.

Here's a short procedure which prints each element starting on a new line:

```
define printitems(list);
vars item;
    for item in list do
        item =>
    endfor;
enddefine;
```

Some people have been known to be confused by the stark clarity of this construction, and find it easier with abstract variable names:

```
define printitems2(l);
vars i;
    for i in l do
        i =>
    endfor;
enddefine;
```

Each time round the loop, the 'looping variable' item (or i) will be set to a different element of list (or l), starting from the front (left, as printed) and going along the list (rightwards), like this:

```
: printitems([a list of things]);
** a
** list
** of
** things
```

The body of the loop won't get executed if the list being looped through doesn't have any elements. And if the expression for the list to be looped through turns out not to be a list, you will get a mishap.

It is instructive to compare the printitems procedure with one written with until: which was the way things were done in the old days, with some early versions of POP-11:

```
define uglyprintitems(list);
    until list = [] do
        hd(list) =>
        tl(list) -> list;
    enduntil;
enddefine;
```

There are many, many, uses for this for construct. Here's just a couple of examples: the first reverses a list, and the second joins two lists together, but without duplicates in the resultant list.

```
define revlist(list) -> result;
vars item;
    [] -> result;
    for item in list do
        item :: result -> result;
    endfor;
enddefine;
```

```
define setjoin(a, b) -> result;
vars item;
    [] -> result;
    for x in a <> b do
        unless member(x, result) then
            x :: result -> result;
        endunless;
    endfor;
enddefine;
```

Numeric Loops

There is no way of completely avoiding numbers; in real life or in programming. Another variant on the for theme executes its body once for each number in a certain range. The syntax is more readily understood by example, so here's a procedure which prints all the numbers from one to ten:

```
define count( );
vars num;
    for num from 1 to 10 do
        num =>
    endfor;
enddefine;
```

For completeness, a description: for, then a variable name, then from, then an expression which evaluates to a number to start from, to, another expression which gives the last value, do, the actions, finally endfor. If the starting value is more than the ending value, then the body of the loop is not executed at all.

This construction has a variant, which makes the number change by a given amount, rather than go up by ones. This procedure prints all the multiples of ten, going down from 100 to –100:

```
define countdown( );
vars num:
    for num from 100 by -10 to -100 do
        num =>
    endfor;
enddefine;
```

You see that after the starting expression, another expression gives the amount to change by, after the keyword by. If you leave this out, as in the previous form, it is the same as having an assumed by 1.

```
define explain (start, incr, limit);
vars num;
    for num from start by incr to limit do
        action( );
    endfor;
    afterwards( );
enddefine;
```

Inevitably, there is some small print. The looping variable doesn't have to land exactly on the end value: it can go past it. And in contrast with other languages, the looping variable has a defined value at the end of the loop. The above is a procedure for reference in the definition.

Definition by example:

1. Evaluate **start, incr** (if present, else assume to be 1), and **limit**. If any of them isn't a number cause a mishap.
2. **start -> num;**
3. If **num** is beyond **limit**, go to step 7.
4. **action();**
5. **num + incr -> num;**
6. Back to step 3.
7. **afterwards();**

Notice that step 5 may decrease **num**, if **incr** is negative. In step 3, 'beyond' means greater than if counting up (**incr** is positive) or less than if counting down (**incr** is negative).

From this definition, you can see that **num** will have a defined value at the end of the loop; that the actions may never get executed; and that infinite loops are possible, such as if **incr** were zero.

Returning from the Middle of a Procedure

Many people consider the best style of procedure to be the one where it starts at the top, at the **define**, works through, and stops when it gets to the **enddefine**. There are cases where this produces procedures which are long or inelegant. POP-11 has the keyword **return**, for procedures which want to terminate in the middle.

Perhaps the best example of a procedure which uses this is the one for finding if a given item is an element of a given list. Of course, this is exactly what the built-in procedure **member** does, but it is worth thinking about how you would write the procedure. It is commonly defined like this:

```
define mem(item, list);
vars element;
    for element in list do
        if item = element then
            return(true);
        endif;
    endfor;
    false;
enddefine;
```

Here, the body of the loop is executed once for each element of the list. It is compared against the argument **item**, and if it is the same, **return** is called with the boolean true. However, if none of the elements equal the **item**, the loop finishes, and we return **false**.

The **return**() causes the termination of the current procedure, as though control had fallen through to the **enddefine**. Syntactically, **return** looks just like a procedure call, although it is in fact a keyword.

Programming Styles

It is a useful exercise to compare various definitions of **mem** and criticise them on points of style. Which of them do you think is the best, and why? Try to form your own opinions before reading the comments which follow the code.

Variations on a Theme

```
define mem1(item, list);
    if list = [] then
        return(false);
    elseif item = hd(list) then
        return(true);
    else
        return(mem1(item, tl(list)));
    endif;
enddefine;

define mem2(item, list);
    until list = [] do
        if hd(list) = item then
            return(true);
        endif;
        tl(list) -> list;
    enduntil;
    false;
enddefine;
define mem3(item, list) -> result;
vars element;
    false -> result;
    for element in list do
        ((item = element) or result) -> result;
    endfor;
enddefine;

define mem4(item, list);
    list /= [] and
    (hd(list) = item or mem4(item, tl(list)));
enddefine;
```

Comments

The first style (mem) is worth examining because it is 'mother-tongue' POP-11 style. Of course, there are accents: some people find the stacking of the **false** at the end confusing, and prefer an explicit **return**. Alternatively, you could define it with an output variable declared on the define line:

```
define mem5(item, list) -> result;
vars element;
    for element in list do
        if item = element then
            true -> result;
            return( );
        endif;
    endfor;
    false -> result;
enddefine;
```

Classic POP-11 recursion is the style of **mem1**: the terminating case first, followed by the success case, followed by the recursive call. The success case also terminates the procedure. The failing case (**list = []**) is first because it is the one which ensures that the procedure terminates. If this was wrong, the procedure might never return. The flow of it is from the more-specific to more-general. You should always try to ensure that your program will have the right kind of control flow, independently of getting the right answers. So, in **mem1**, you can see that it will recurse down the list by the call

```
mem1(..., tl(list))
```

in the **else** clause. As we know that **list** is the argument, we know that the recursive call will always have a shorter argument list than the caller. Secondly, the procedure immediately returns (before any fiddling with its arguments) if it is given an empty list. For a short procedure like this, things are clear enough. More complicated procedures should follow these rules more rigidly, as they are harder to fix if they get bugs. Finally, because the control structure is correct, the rest of the code follows naturally. Most recursive procedures which manipulate lists do so like this one. It is also quite a common LISP style, and would look like this:

```
(defun mem1 (item lst)
    (cond ((null lst) nil)
          ((eq item (car lst)) t)
          (t (mem1 item (cdr lst)))))
```

Iterative control is the major control structure found in other languages, and is often used in POP-11. Most iterative list-manipulating procedures look like **mem**, but sometimes it is necessary to use the simple **until** or **while** rather than **for**. A case in point is where two lists have to be manipulated at the same time. The procedure **mem2** isn't really as good as **mem**, but is included to show you another way of doing the same thing.

Programmers from other languages are often startled by procedures like **mem3**. It shows that you can use boolean operators such as **or** in other places than as conditions for **if**s and **while**s and their friends. They behave just like ordinary procedures. It has to be said that many POP-11 programmers don't like this sort of use. It also has some syntactic quirks which make the placing of brackets even more important than usual: the example has 'full' brackets. You are advised to err on the side of caution too.

The last example is POP-11 with a PROLOG accent. We have written a boolean expression which expresses the truth of the assertion that the item is in the list. The trick for this kind of procedure is to think of POP-11 as evaluating expressions, rather than executing code. It is clearer in LISP than POP-11, because LISP has uniform syntax, so **and** and the others look just like any other expression:

```
(defun em4 (item lst)
       (and (not (eq lst ()))
            (or  (eq item (car lst))
                 (mem4 item (cdr lst)))))))
```

(For non-LISP programmers: **car** means **hd** and **cdr** means **tl**.)

In both LISP and POP-11, the order that you check the cases is critical in procedures like this. This is because **and** and **or** work their arguments out from left to right, and don't bother to evaluate parts which they know don't affect the answer. For example,

```
: true or false =>
** <true>
: true or true =>
** <true>
```

Here you see that if the left-most thing evaluates to <true>, **or** doesn't have to evaluate the right-hand one, as the answer will be the same. The procedure only works because we don't have to evaluate the recursive call to **mem4** when one of the simpler cases on the left determines its answer.

This idea of regarding procedures as expressions is most common in mathematics and logic, and is how most programs are written in PROLOG. The classic PROLOG example is of inherited properties, such as being a descendant of someone. In English, you might define being a descendant thus: 'someone is your descendant if they are your child, or your child's child, or your child's child's child, and so on.' Being more formal, as POP-11 doesn't (yet) understand 'and so on': someone is your descendant if they are your child, or the descendant of a child. The procedure then is like a programmed series of questions to ask to see if someone is a descendant or not. Roughly speaking, tl is like 'child', mem4 would mean 'descendant of' and the checking against [] is like 'is older than'. For comparison, this is how mem4 would look in PROLOG:

```
mem4(Item, [Item|_] ).
mem4(Item, [_|Tail]) :-
    mem4(Item, Tail).
```

(For non-PROLOG programmers: [...|...] breaks a list up into the head and the tail. The first clause of the POP-11 and LISP versions isn't needed in PROLOG, because there is an implicit 'is non-empty list' in the brackets notation.)

Summary

The presentation of different styles of programming here is to help you get used to some of the techniques which POP-11 programmers use. Some of them have been imported from other languages, and some of them are useful only rarely.

For this particular case, the first definition (mem) is probably the best. Iteration is (computationally) cheaper than recursion, and there is no complexity penalty for using it here. In general, using for is better than using until or while, as the code will be easier to read and shorter – and you can't forget the tl(list) -> list;

Of the recursive styles, mem1 is the most used. If you have to write a procedure which tells if a given object is a member of a given list, or any sublist of it, you should start from mem1. You won't get anywhere if you start from mem. The PROLOG-style mem4 should show you that you can often simplify if-statements into much shorter expressions.

Exercises B

1. Write procedures to add up a list of numbers. See how many different ways you can do it.
2. Write a procedure to see if a given item is in a nested list, at any depth. It should behave like this:

```
: anymem("hello", []) =>
** <false>
: anymem("hello", [x y hello z]) =>
** <true>

: anymem("hello", [x [y [hello]] z]) =>
** <true>
```

3. Write a procedure to add up all the numbers in a nested list. So you could get 20 from addnested([1 [3 2] [4 [5 6] -1]]).

CHAPTER 6

Review

Having worked this far through the text, you should be in a position to write your own procedures which cope with most problems. Obviously, there is a way yet to go: this chapter describes some high-level ideas behind programming in POP-11, and gives some suggestions for programs you might write to practice your skills.

What is a POP-11 Program?

In some languages, such as PASCAL, there is a syntactically defined structure called the 'program', which comprises the totality of some program. In POP-11, the concept is more amorphous. Textually, a program consists of all the definitions for your procedures and data structures. Normally you want to keep your programs, and so you should write them in an editor program, which makes files which stay on your system. This problem arises because POP-11 is an interactive, dynamic language: and, in present implementations, is compiled. POP-11 doesn't keep the source form of your procedures, it just keeps its own internal representation.

One of the great benefits of the POPLOG system is that it has a very powerful screen editor which makes a lot of the chores in writing programs disappear. You can flick from writing a procedure to trying a different one to inspecting some output to reading documentation. Other POP-11 systems have editors of one kind or another: or you can use any editor which you have on your system.

The usual convention is to put POP-11 programs in files which show they are in POP-11. The classic method is used, so that the names look like, for example, foo.p, but different operating systems have different concepts for this. On Unix and Macintosh systems you give them filenames which end with .p, under VMS or MS-DOS systems you would give them a file extension of p. In any case, you type the dot, and the system will print it when it lists your files.

Once such a file exists, you can bring it into play by 'loading' it. This compiles it, or reads it into memory, or whatever is needed by your system to make it runnable. In essence, it is as though you just typed it all in again. Suppose you have a file called exercises.p, which contains all of your answers for questions in this book, and you want to load it in again. Simple:

```
: load exercises.p;
;;; LOADING exercises.p
```

Of course, on different systems you might get a different message, or none at all, indicating what's going on. For example, on the Macintosh, you can give load commands with the mouse, and the cursor changes while the program loads.

If your file is big, loading could take some time. When it is finished loading, you'll get your prompt back.

As mentioned above, loading a file is just like pretending to type its contents to POP-11: so if there are any mistakes or problems with it, you'll get a mishap message. When this happens, you'll have to edit your file to fix the problem, and try loading it again. Also, if any parts of your file print things out or run procedures, that happens when you load your file.

Because of this, people normally put just the procedure definitions and variable declarations in their files. The calls to the procedures are normally typed in afterwards. A common way to do it is to have a procedure defined in the file called start or setup or something similar, or something related to the name of the program. Imagine a parsing program, in a file called parse.p, whose initial procedure is called parse which takes a list of words to parse. Then you might do this:

```
: load parse.p;
;;; LOADING parse.p
: parse([the dog]) =>
** [nounphrase [det the] [noun dog]]
```

People also write comments in the files: you can write these anywhere, and there are two forms. The first is for brief comments: any text between three semicolons and the end of a line is ignored by POP-11. The second is for longer texts: anything between /* and its matching */ is ignored. A procedure with some commenting:

```
/* demonstration of comments in front of
 * a procedure which doesn't do anything interesting
 */
define boring();
[yawn] = > ;;; just print the message
enddefine;
```

The asterisk on the second line isn't needed, but is a common style to make the comment stand out. A point to watch: the 'slash-star' comments nest: that is, you can comment out a comment with them:

```
/* anything here
    /* anything here too
    a comment: i thought the fireworks were good
    */
    and and anything here as well
*/
```

Each /* matches its *own* */, not the next one.

One of the biggest problems in programming is documentation. Suppose you have lots of programs: how do you remember how to use each one? One good way is to have a documentation file to go with each program: ours would be parse.doc perhaps. Then you can write down how to invoke each program, what it does, doesn't do, and so on. Don't be too proud to write a description of limitations and bugs.

Every programming textbook is obliged to say:

'The importance of documentation cannot be over stressed. Every program will be altered, often by someone else. Even programs which you think will only be used by yourself should be documented, because if you have to go back to a program you wrote a year ago, it is almost certain that you will have forgotten how it works.'

The same remarks also apply to comments within your program. Liberal commenting makes programming easier. It is so easy to forget the constraints on some variable, or the inputs to some procedure. Try to get into the habit of writing a few lines of comment above *every* procedure. Describe the purpose of the procedure, the representations it expects in its arguments, what the result means, and so on. Describe each global variable in the same way. It is also good to put comments describing the use of the program. And always put your name and the date on programs.

Libraries

The only way civilisation develops is by building on those who have gone before: programming included. Hence, POP-11 has a library mechanism. Library files in POP-11 are just like ordinary files, except that they are shared by all the users of a system, thus saving people reinventing the wheel all the time. They reside in library directories, and the POP-11 system knows where there are.

How files get into the library is an operating system and implementation issue; getting documentation on them is the same. Specifying where the libraries are is another. But using the library is straightforward; instead of load use lib.

On a system which has no hard disks you may have to juggle some floppy disks around.

POP-11 also has an 'autoloadable library'. This is a mechanism for loading definitions of procedures and variables automatically when needed. The reasoning behind this is that you can make a procedure seem as though it is built-in, but it only actually gets defined if you try to use it. You do not have to do anything to make use of the autoloadable library – it just happens.

Operating System and Implementation Issues

There are several basic issues which are so dependent on operating systems and implementations that they are not discussed at length in this book.

Documentation

The most important is the documentation of the system. The description of procedures and features of POP-11 in this book are general: but of course every implementation has variations, extensions, additions – and bugs. And things which depend on your operating system are different on different host computers.

You will have to read through and become familiar with the documentation which comes with your system – there is no other source of definitive information on your implementation. And you will need to be on at least nodding terms with your operating system, in order to log in, delete files, copy things, and so on.

Your documentation may be printed, or it might be online, or both. If it is online, as in POPLOG, you get at it with the keyword **help**, appropriately enough. Once you are in the help system, it should give you information on how to get out.

Specifically for POPLOG users:
If you see a colon prompt, just type **help** and press return. If you don't see a colon prompt, ask someone how to get into the help system.

If your system isn't POPLOG, you could still try that and see what happens.

Editor

The second most important is the editor you use to write your programs in. You will have to investigate the documentation on your system to find out about it.

POP-11 is designed to be an interactive system, and so modern implementations have a built-in editor. You can make new files, change old ones, just look at them, and so on. But you can also run programs in them, make new definitions, and load parts of files. To get the most from any programming system, it really helps to be very familiar with the editor, which is probably the part of the system you will spend most time using.

Specifically for POPLOG users:
In reality, the editor is the same as the help system, and is called VED. Learn to use the help system, and you will have learnt how to use VED. You get into the editor from the colon prompt by typing just **ved** and pressing return. To edit a file of a given name, for example **foo.p**, just type
: **ved** foo.p

You can edit any number of files at the same time, and switch between them as you need to.

Specifically for POP-11 on Macintoshes:

In common with most other Macintosh software, you get into the editor by pulling down the FILE menu. You click the mouse on NEW to edit a new file, or OPEN to edit an old one. The editor is quite conventional: anyone familiar with Macintosh software will have no trouble using it. You can edit many files at the same time, and switch between them as you like, so long as you have enough memory.

Library Files

It is possible to make your own libraries, and to put your own files in the standard libraries.

Adding to the standard libraries is different depending on your system. If you share your system with other people, you should talk to your system manager, who is in charge (or will know who is) of the libraries. If your system is single-user, read your documentation: you are in charge. (A warning: don't ever alter the disks or tapes your system came on.)

Making your own libraries is dependent on your implementation: you will probably have to change some built-in variable. Check the documentation.

Other Operating System Issues

Essentially operating systems are concerned with resource management and the user interface. POP-11 systems rely on operating systems to manipulate files, find out the time, control terminals or screens, and so on. And practically every one of these will have limitations and effects on what POP-11 can do. Even the 'same system', if it runs on different operating systems, will be subtly different. Here are a few tips:

Filenames: Different operating systems have different rules for filenames. Some consider A and a to be the same; some have limits on the allowable length; some won't let you use certain characters, and so on. Filenames tend not to be portable: the best advice is to put file names in variables, and then they will be easy to change. If you need to have filenames portable across different operating systems, here are some tips: begin with a letter, use only lowercase letters, have a dot in the name, with at most eight characters before it, and at most three after. For example: joe5.old

Files: It should be possible in your system to find out things like the length of a particular file, or what files you have, from within POP-11. Such things tend to differ greatly across operating systems and implementations.

Time: You should be able to find out the time from within POP-11: don't count on this being portable across implementations. You may find several ways in a given implementation, some of which it maintains across operating systems, some of which is doesn't.

Terminal: You will be able to control the screen and read the keyboard from POP-11, but the facilities and how to work them are entirely dependent on the hardware you have. For example, Macintoshes have a mouse, but terminals connected to VAXes usually don't. And people connect all kinds of terminals to VAXes and other multiuser systems. You will have to trade off control against portability in programs which want to have close control of hardware like this.

Size of Programs: Clearly, a microcomputer with 128 kilobytes of memory won't be able to run as big a program as a minicomputer which fills a room and has virtual memory, hard disks and dozens of megabytes of main memory. Also, it probably won't go as fast. There is no way out of this problem: it is the reason why there are different kinds of computers.

Implementation Issues

To some degree, implementation issues overlap with operating system issues: you can't get all operating systems on all computers. But more importantly, different implementations have different design goals. And, currently, there is no standard for implementations other than that provided by the dominant implementation: POPLOG. At the time of writing, POP-11 for Macintoshes is still being developed; and POP-11 for Digital PDP11 minicomputers is all but obsolete. Other implementations have been written in universities and some companies, but are not commercially available.

The features and procedures described in this book are those which should be available on every system: they are the ones most commonly used. Every system will offer others as well; for instance to interface to the operating system.

Typical issues in portability are:

Data types supported. Some of the fancier data types may not exist on all implementations.

Built-in procedures. Some implementations have more built-in procedures than others. Functionality of a given procedure may differ on two implementations. Of particular importance are generality, options, and bugs.

Library Programs. Big systems have big libraries. The same issues as for built-in features – although normally the problem is purely one of what is available.

Autoloading. On a computer with only floppy disks, autoloading is very slow. Implementors will therefore tend away from putting things in the autoloadable library. On a big system, autoloadable libraries can be very attractive. To some extent, therefore, whether a given procedure is built-in or autoloadable is an implementation decision. Otherwise, the same comments as for library programs.

Control Mechanisms. POP-11 is a flexible language, and so you are able to control the way it works. For example, there might be a variable which tells the system to print objects in a different way; on some other system you might have to call a procedure.

Exercise Programs

You should spend some time practising your programming: the only way to learn is by doing. The best thing is to set yourself a task, and write a program for it. Of course, the kind of program you will be able to tackle will depend on how much programming experience you have. The following list of suggestions is roughly in order of difficulty: if you have written programs which do similar things in other languages you'll obviously have less trouble. The figures in brackets give a rough guess of how many lines the program might be. Brackets indicate the discipline which the project is about; (maths), (engineering) and so on.

You should write the programs in your editor, keeping in mind the suggestions made earlier about comments, indentation, and other stylistic aspects. If possible, you should find a kindly soul who is familiar with POP-11 to give your programs a read once you've done them – comments from an experienced programmer are invaluable. The exercises up to 10 have answers and hints.

1. Write a procedure which substitutes items in a list. It should work like this:

   ```
   : subst("dog", "cat", [the cat sat on the mat]) =>
   ** [the dog sat on the mat]
   ```
   (10)

2. A procedure which counts the number of occurrences of a specific item in a list:

   ```
   : count("dog", [the dog really is a dog]) =>
   ** 2
   ```
   (10)

3. A procedure which counts the number of lists in a list:

   ```
   : countlists([nounphrase [det the] [noun dog]]) =>
   ** 2
   ```
   (10)

4. A procedure which adds up all the numbers in a list:

   ```
   : totlist([1 2 3 4 100]) =>
   ** 110
   ```
   (10)

Can you make it work for the list [1 ein 2 zwei]? What result should it give? There are lots of rules which your program could use for this: one rule gives 3, another gives

10, another gives 9. In a language where data types are mixed freely, there is more thinking to do before selecting what is the 'right answer' for many procedures. A good exercise is to find as many different, good, rules as you can. Try to abstract from your answers the criteria which you might use to select one for any given purpose. Of course, you might regard the best answer as being 6. How would you set about writing a program which could get this answer? Such programs can be very complex and large: ask yourself how many languages you can read numbers in, and how you do it.

5. (Maths) A procedure which calculates factorials. (The factorial of a positive whole number is 1 times 2 times 3 times all the numbers up to the given number. The factorial of zero is 1. Factorials of negative and fractional numbers are not defined.) Try to make your procedure do something sensible for results which aren't defined. Find out the biggest number that your system will let you take the factorial of. (10)

6. (Holidays) Write a program which is a simple lexicon for some foreign language. Probably a good idea is to limit it to buying things, or talking to dentists, or hotel keepers. Think carefully about your data representation: will it let you translate in both directions? (30–100+)

7. (Statistics) Write a set of procedures for working out statistics. Start with a procedure for finding the average of a list of numbers.

8. Write a procedure for sorting a list of things into ascending length. What kinds of things can your procedure deal with? Try writing several procedures which sort by different algorithms. (Note: POP-11 has a built-in procedure called **sort**, so call yours something else: it is still a valuable exercise if you've never done it before.) (20+)

9. (Maths/logic) Write a set of procedures for manipulating sets, represented as lists without duplications. You should include procedures for finding the intersection of two sets (a set of all the objects common to both sets); the union (all the objects in either); for discovering whether some object is in a set; for adding and removing things from a set; for finding all the elements of one set which aren't in another set. (30)

10. (Cooking/holidays) A program for converting imperial units to metric, or one currency to another. You should be able to give it a list like [254 mm] and get [10 inches]. (20+)

11. A program to play noughts and crosses (tic-tac-toe). (80+)

12. Kriegspiel chess is like the normal game, except that each player's pieces are invisible to their opponents. This game requires an umpire who can see all the pieces, to disallow moves which break the rules: make a program which is the umpire and

boards. An additional rule says that players may ask the umpire if they can take any
pieces with their pawns.   (200+)

13. Othello is a game where one move can mean you have to turn lots of pieces over,
which slows it down. Write a program which is an 'intelligent' board for this game,
and turns over the pieces when needed. Briefly, the rules are these: there are two
players, black and white, an 8 × 8 board, and 64 pieces which are white on one side
and black on the other. Start with the board as shown: white plays first. The players
take it in turn to put a piece down with their own colour upwards. You can only put
a piece down if it will be one end of a straight line (including diagonals) which has
your colour at each end and some of your opponent's in the middle: and you get to
turn these over. So white can start at E6 and turn over the black piece at E5. If you
can't go because you can't turn over any pieces, you just skip your turn. When the
board is full or neither player can go, the game ends: the winner is the player with the
most of their colour showing.

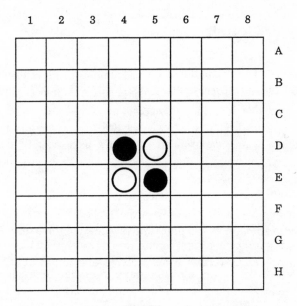

Fig. 6.1

14. (Engineering) Dimensional analysis is a process which manipulates representations of measurements. Write a program which converts representations to their
canonical form. For example, you may have a volume represented as [100 m m m],
and want to divide it by a length represented as [20 m], to get the result [5 m m].
How should you represent 'metres per second'? You could make your program
convert Centimetre-Gramme-Second units into SI units, or vice versa. Or take

measurements in any units, and give the result in SI or CGS units.   (100–1000)

15. A concordance is a lexicon of a text which says which words are used, how many times, and (sometimes) where. Write a program which gives a concordance of a list. Find a way of making it ignore uninteresting words such as 'the' and 'a'. (50–200)

16. Write a program for manipulating names, addresses and phone numbers. If you have the hardware (a modem) you could think about how to make it dial your friends.   (50+)

17. (Maths) You can represent vectors and arrays in lists: implement some procedures for the usual vector functions of addition, subtraction, dot product, cross product and multiplication by a scalar. Do the same for arrays for the functions of addition, subtraction, multiplication, inversion and determinant evaluation. (Note: POP-11 has data types called 'vectors' and 'arrays' which are covered later: they would be more efficient for this task. You may like to do this project both with lists and the other types, or postpone it until reading about them.) Your arrays might look like this:

[[1 2 3] [4 5 6] [7 8 9]]   A 3 × 3 array.

                                                                        (100+)

18. A game, called 'life', involves single cell animals living in a petri dish. The petri dish is divided into little squares, like graph paper, and the cells will only form on the crosses. Each cell therefore has eight neighbours: North, NE, E, SE, S, SW, W, NW. All the cells form or die once a second, in synchrony. These cells must have at least two neighbours, or they die of loneliness (at the next second); and not more than three, or they die of overcrowding. A vacant cell with exactly three neighbours is formed at the next second. Write a program which lets you put down an initial array of cells, and prints out the colony pattern for each generation. This game was devised by the mathematician John Conway in the 1960s, and has become infamous for consuming vast amounts of computer and programmer time since then; don't make your petri dish too big.   (100)

19. (Linguistics) A representation for parse trees has been shown in an earlier chapter. Write a parser for a simple CF grammar. Perhaps extend this to do simple translations to a foreign language. Perhaps write a generator, which shows all possibilities of your grammar.   (100+)

20. (Computer Science) POP-11 is very similar to LISP: it has lists, its words correspond to LISP's atoms. Write a tiny LISP interpreter.   (20–100)

CHAPTER 7

Control and the Stack Again

One of the key ways in which POP-11 differs from other similar languages is its method of passing data around on the stack. While it is possible to go quite a long way without fully understanding the stack, you will always bump into limits unless you master it. The 'naive' view of the stack is purely as an implementation detail for how to get arguments and results from A to B. However, you will see that there are a great many useful applications for the stack in its own right, which make it invaluable for expressing some procedures. Of course, there is a downside too: and certain bugs may arise which can be difficult to track down.

Non-destructive Assignment

Many a program has been written which expresses: 'get data and process it and keep going until there is no more data'. How cleanly can this be written in POP-11? There is a problem here, because you really have two actions with a test in between, and there is no natural POP-11 looping construct for this. One common solution is like this:

```
define foo();
vars x;
    getdata() -> x;
    while x do
        processdata(x);
        getdata() -> x;
    endwhile;
enddefine;
```

Which of course relies on some arbitrary **getdata** and **processdata** procedures for getting and processing the information. The assumed representation is that when **getdata** returns <false> it means that it can't get any more data.

The thing that is ugly about this procedure is that there are two calls to **getdata**: one to initialise the loop, and another to keep it going. The *only* case where that would be good style is if getting the first piece of data was in some way different from getting later ones. In order to make this kind of procedure (and many others) easier, POP-11 has a 'non-destructive' assignment arrow, which leaves the stack unchanged:

87

remember that the ordinary one removes the top item from the stack. It is formed as
a double-headed assignment arrow: ->>, and would be used like this:

```
define nicefoo( );
vars x;
    while getdata( ) ->> x do
        processdata(x);
    endwhile
enddefine;
```

As you can see, getting the data is now performed in a single place in the procedure
as is appropriate.

A note about syntax: the double-headed assignment expression sometimes needs
to be put into brackets. The syntax rules for this are covered elsewhere: for the
present, just remember this idiom, which is how it is often used:

```
until (getdata( ) ->> x) = nil do
    ...
enduntil;
```

A note about the VM: it is instructive to look at the virtual machine instructions for
the double-headed assignment arrow. Remembering that a normal assignment is just
a POP, the double-headed version just pushes again afterwards:

```
123 -> x;                        123 ->> x;
POP        "x"                    POP         "x"
                                 PUSH        "x"
```

Which is exactly what is needed in the nicefoo procedure: because we want to keep
the result of getdata in the variable x, so we can use it again; and we need the value
of the data for the while to test.

Procedures with Many Results

The most common procedures have either one or no results. The ones with no results
usually print things out, or start programs off, and so on. Most procedures which do
'real work' present the product of the work as a procedure result. This is at the nub
of structured programming, because it means you can write procedures without
knowing which other procedures will call them, and similarly, you can write
procedures which call another one without having (yet) written the called procedure.

Sometimes, it becomes difficult to express your procedure clearly with just a single
result. An example of this might be a procedure which takes the name of a person and
gives back both the parents' names.

There is some methodological debate about this: perhaps you should return a representation of the person, which would contain both parents' names, rather than the two items. We shall bypass this debate, because there are some important uses for multiple result procedures, which will be shown presently.

Here is a definition for such a procedure:

```
define parentsof(name) -> father -> mother;
    if name = "jonathan" then
        "jules" -> father;
        "helen" -> mother;
    else
        false -> father;
        false -> mother;
    endif;
enddefine;
```

An aside: we could have written

```
false ->>> father -> mother;
```

Notice the define line has two assignments: it is a definition for a statement of the form:

```
: parentsof(...) -> ... -> ... ;
```

Why is this possible? Returning a result is just a case of pushing an object onto the stack at the end of the procedure. Because the stack is 'open', there is nothing to stop you pushing more than one thing. Usually, the alternative to a procedure like the one shown above is to have two procedures, one for the mother and one for the father, and then invoking them like this:

```
: vars ma pa;
: fatherof("jonathan") -> pa;
: motherof("jonathan") -> ma;
```

For purposes of explanation, we will use a simpler example:

```
: "jules" -> pa;
: "helen" -> ma;
```

Examined in terms of the virtual machine, we are pushing the two names, and popping them into the two variables. (In the version with the procedures, we just had to do more work to get the parents' names on the stack.) In VM instructions, it is this:

```
PUSHQ     "jules"
POP       "pa"
PUSHQ     "helen"
POP       "ma"
```

Of course, that isn't the only way to skin this cat:

```
PUSHQ      "helen"
PUSHQ      "jules"
POP        "pa"
POP        "ma"
```

You can see that it is possible to reverse the order of the PUSH instructions, and do all the pushing and then all the popping.

This is exactly what the procedure **parentsof** does: the declaration ... -> father -> mother; makes POP-11 put two objects on the stack at the end of the procedure. This is done so that the leftmost one in the definition (**father**) will be on the top of the stack at the end – it is pushed last.

As mentioned before, some people regard procedures like this to be unstructured, poor design; for some it is a style question; for others it is perfectly good technique.

Variable Number of Results

In POP-11, you will find that having a variable number of results is much more useful than simply a fixed, plural, number. All that is needed is some way for your program to control how many things get pushed by a procedure, and you can make a variable number of results for your procedures.

Of course, at the base level, everything in POP-11 which isn't a definition, a control structure, a procedure call, or an assignment is a push.

Just to recap: apart from keywords like **define** and **while**, almost all of POP-11 consists of assignments, procedure calls, object references, and variable references. (Actually, assignment is just a normal keyword too.)

Apart from the keywords, POP-11 has trivial rules for how to execute things:

1. Executing a procedure call means executing all the text between the parentheses, then invoking the procedure with a **CALL** virtual machine instruction.
2. Executing an object reference means building the object, and then pushing it.
3. Executing a variable reference means pushing the value of the variable.
   So, to the code: here's a procedure which pushes ten empty lists:

```
define empties();
    repeat 10 times
        [];
    endrepeat;
enddefine;
```

And easy to test, remembering that the print arrow (when at the colon prompt) prints all the objects on the stack, leaving it empty:

```
: empties( ) >
** [] [] [] [] [] [] [] [] [] []
```

This may not look very useful, because we have not yet any method of doing anything with these objects other than have ten assignments, or some number of procedure calls.

Making a List from Multiple Results

The single most useful thing to do with lots of results on the stack is to collect them up into a list. As it is so useful, it has special syntax, called 'decorated list brackets', made from percent signs.

Using the **empties** procedure of the previous section, we can easily make a list of ten empty lists:

```
: [% empties( ); %] =>
** [[] [] [] [] [] [] [] [] [] []]
```

At any point in a list, you can have a 'decorated' section, which consists of a percent sign, some ordinary POP-11 text, and another percent sign. Remember that normally between list brackets all the words are just taken to be elements of the list you are making. But in a decorated section, the words are taken to be normal POP-11, like the procedure call to **empties** in the example.

Inside a decorated section, the procedure calls (or whatever) are executed, and any items left on the stack are put into the list you are making. Usually there is only one decorated section in a list, but you can have any number. Think of the decorated sections as 'procedural' list making, and the undecorated parts as 'declarative'. In the first a program decides what's in the list; in the second you have to write out explicitly every item that you want. The formal terminology is that the decorated parts are 'evaluated', while the other parts are 'unevaluated'.

Here's a procedure for making a list of numbers up to some limit, followed by a few words:

```
define hideandseek(n);
vars i;
    [% for i from 1 to n do
             n;
         endfor; % ready or not here i come];
enddefine;
```

Notice the undecorated section at the end of the list, which just gives some words we want in the list; the decorated part at the front has a numeric for loop to generate the numbers.

Exercises

1. Rewrite this procedure using decorated lists:

```
define glue(left, right);
   [^left ^right];
enddefine;
```

Sometimes, the simplest cases are harder to see. Think about this next procedure. Note that it uses an explicit result variable, just for variation.

```
define gluetails(left, right) -> glued;
vars lefttail righttail;
    tl(left) -> lefttail;
    tl(right) -> righttail;
    [^lefttail ^righttail] -> glued;
enddefine;
```

2. Look at this procedure:
```
define bug(list);
vars tail;
    until (tl(list) -> tail) = [] do
         tail;
    enduntil;
enddefine;
```

   (a) What is wrong with it?
   (b) What does it do?
   (c) Change it so that it returns only one result.

CHAPTER 8

Data Structures

Data Objects

This chapter explains in detail the structure of the objects we've met so far. The next chapter covers the unifying concept behind the data classes: the key. The subsequent chapter describes the remaining data types. On a first read, you might like to just skim the section on numbers in this chapter, and skip the chapter on further types altogether. But you should definitely read the next chapter. It comes after this one, so that you will have an understanding of the mechanisms underlying all of POP-11's manipulations on structures.

Data Classes

Every data object is said to belong to a single 'class', which is an abstraction of the sameness of all the objects of what is usually called 'the same data type'. The primitives from which all data actions are built are very clear in POP-11, and there are generic actions which can be performed on any data object whatsoever. Readers familiar with object-oriented programming will recognise many concepts: what we have is a mechanism for defining methods for certain operations on certain classes.

The actions and how they are performed is the subject of the next chapter. Briefly, the operations are these: they can be *constructed*, to make another; *printed*, so you can see them; *compared for equality*; *recognised*, as being of a given class; *applied*, so expressions such as **x( )** are defined; *accessed*, so you can take them apart.

Simple and Compound Objects

POP-11 has two basic kinds of object. The first is a 'simple' object, and the second is 'compound'. Almost all the data types are compound.

The distinction rests on an implementation detail. A compound object resides in memory, and is always referred to by its 'address'. A simple object can be anywhere, and is always referred to by its value.

Normally, small whole numbers (and sometimes others as well) are represented as simples. Words would always be a compound type. Suppose we had two variables,

93

foo and baz:

```
: vars foo baz;
: 45 -> foo;
: "hello" -> baz;
```

Here we have three words (two are the names of variables) and one number. Each word is represented as a place in memory, as in Figure 8.1. The numbers on the right represent the 'address' of each word. In this diagram, each word has three parts: its name, its address, and the value of the variable it names (in the box). Every word could be the name of a variable, and so has a box. You see that hello has no value, so its box has a line through it. You see foo has the value 45, and baz has as its value the address of hello.

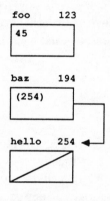

Fig. 8.1

Why is the address of hello in parentheses? POP-11 must have some way of telling that the 254 is an address, not the number 254: in the diagram this is shown by parentheses. Distinguishing simples and compounds is a classical problem for implementing languages like this: often it is done by limiting the range of numbers (or other simples) which can be represented, and then making compounds have huge numbers for addresses.

All that you need to understand is that POP-11 represents some objects as pointers, and some as a coding of the object directly. The choice is dependent on many intricate factors: in general, things like numbers are simples; everything else is compound.

What is the point of this? Most structures are intricate, and have a lot of components. For example, if comparing two words involved comparing all the letters in them all the time, everything would be very slow. Instead, because words (being compound objects) are always referred to by their address, it simply suffices to compare addresses. In the example above, comparing hello with baz is very simple: compare the addresses 254 and 194. As they are different, so are the words.

This introduces a new concept of 'identity'. We say that two objects are identical if they have the same address, or they are the same simple. Simples are never identical to compounds, and there must always be a method of distinguishing them. Notice that this is different from the concept of 'equality' defined in a previous chapter, which was that two objects were equal if they were of the same type, and if appropriate, same length and equal contents. It should be clear that any two objects which are identical will also be equal. POP-11 has an infix operator for testing identity, which is formed from two equals signs: try not to mix it up with the equals symbol.

If you experiment with the identity operator, you will quickly discover that very few things are identical:

```
: 2 == 2 =>
** <true>
: [hello] == [hello] =>
** <false>

: "hello" == "hello"=>
** <true>
```

As identity is not an intuitive concept, these are the data types met so far where identity and equality are always the same: words, booleans, procedures.

Unless you have met this idea before, such as in LISP, you may find it troublesome. The best advice is to always use equality tests until you're more sure of it. The following sections on different data types explain their structures in more detail, and so will shed some light on identity and equality for them.

The point of identity is that it is a very primitive and fast operation for the computer to test. The equals procedure is written in terms of identity.

POP-11 has a number of unique objects, which are built in and which you can't make more of. These include the boolean objects, the special empty list, and a few others.

To summarise, all POP-11 objects are either simple or compound. Simple objects are always referred to by their value, and are exemplified by small whole numbers. Compound objects are structures in memory, and are always referred to by the address of the structure. All objects which can refer to other objects are compound, and have 'cells' which contain the references. Comparing objects with identity might be convenient for POP-11, but is often problematic for programmers.

Lists

Lists are actually implemented in terms of another data type: the pair. Pairs are actually very rarely used except for this purpose, but you will find an understanding of them useful for manipulating lists. There is also, as you will remember, a special 'empty list', which is also known as nil. This is a special object, which means that it is not like any other object. The name is a hangover from LISP systems, and most POP programmers prefer to use its other form, which refers to exactly the same object: [].

A pair is a structure which can contain two objects, referred to as the front and the back of the pair. A list is either the special 'empty list', or is a construction of pairs, where the back of each pair points to another pair, or to the empty list.

The list [one two three] is represented in Figure 8.2. Each box represents one pair, with its front on the left, and its back on the right. In this diagram, you see that there are pointers in each cell: the backs all point to other pairs, except the last, which points to []. The fronts all point to words.

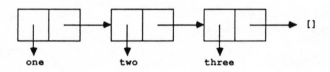

Fig. 8.2

As should be familiar, the tail of this list is [two three], and the tail of that is [three] and the tail of that is []. You should be able to recognise these structures in Figure 8.2. It's obvious that in some way fronts correspond to heads, and backs correspond to tails – but how?

The answer is simple: every (non-empty) list is made up of pairs, the same number of pairs as there are elements of the list. The front of the first pair will be the head of the list, and the back of it will be the tail. But the procedures for manipulating lists do some extra checking to make sure that you have a good list, and not some arbitrary structure made of pairs – for example, that shown in Figure 8.3. While it is a perfectly good structure, in the sense that it is allowed in POP-11, it isn't a list. This is because its back doesn't contain a pair, and doesn't contain []. If you tried to take its hd you would get a mishap message.

Fig. 8.3

How do the list operations work? We've already seen what lists look like in terms of pairs and [], and seen how the heads and tails work in terms of fronts and backs of pairs. What about cons, the procedure for joining lists?

Consider this:

```
: vars list;
: [] -> list;
```

In 'box diagram' form, it looks like Figure 8.4. Suppose we cons a word on the front:

```
: "hello" :: list -> list;
: list =>
** [hello]
```

Now it looks like Figure 8.5.

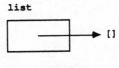

Fig. 8.4

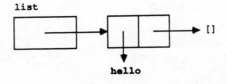

Fig. 8.5

The cons procedure (::) had two arguments, the first of which was a pointer to the word hello, and the second a pointer to []. Cons's job is to check first that its second argument is a list. As it is it passes the test. Then it builds a new pair, and puts its two arguments in it. Then it returns the new list as its result, which we assigned back into the variable list.

Let's continue with this structure, and add some more variables, like this:

```
: vars another;
: "bonjour" :: list -> another;
: another =>
  ** [bonjour hello]
: vars different;
: [hello] -> different;
```

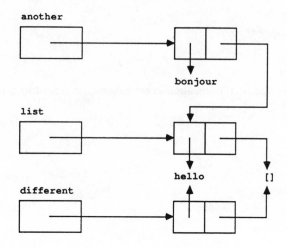

Fig. 8.6

Cons goes through its routine again, and a list is built for the variable **different**: now the picture looks like Figure 8.6. You see that, as requested, cons built another pair and put all the things in the right place. And you see that the tail of the list in **another** is the same as the list in the variable **list**. In fact, as you can see from the diagram, they are identical. But the list in the variable **different** is completely disconnected from the other lists. Now you should be able to see the difference between two lists being equal, and them being identical. The tail of **another** is *identical* to the list in **list**; both of these are *equal* to the list in **different**, but not identical. The only way for structures to be identical is for them to be the same structure, or made from the same structure, as **another** was made from **list**. This is because POP-11 builds structures on demand, as it did with **different**.

Why are lists implemented this way, out of pairs? The answer is really about efficiency for various tasks. You can see from the process illustrated above that lists sometimes share common tails. This makes some processes very efficient, in particular the lengthening of a list in a variable, as we did with **list** above. It can also be very convenient for structures to share data.

Be warned, however, it can also be dangerous *in the extreme*. As has often been remarked, some of the wickedest bugs in POP-11 (and LISP) arise from misunderstandings on this subject. You are advised to steer well clear of writing programs which, for example, change the heads or tails of lists, or use the fact that lists sometimes share parts. Usually, it is better to regard the sharing as just an efficiency trick which the system sometimes does to speed things up. Programs which require these kinds of structures are rare; and there are plenty of other features of POP-11 which are much more useful, and should be learned first.

Other Data Types

Having gone into the stucture of lists in some detail, the other structures should be very straightforward.

Only lists, words, numbers, booleans and procedures are presented in this chapter. Keys are discussed in Chapter 9. The remaining types are presented in Chapter 10.

Lists (to recap) are used to collect objects together, in an ordered sequence. You can make lists of any objects whatsoever. A list of lists is called a 'nested list'. There is an empty list, the unique object **[]**. Lists are made whenever needed, so equality is not the same as identity. They are especially useful if you need to have a collection of objects which might get bigger or smaller. Lists are made from pairs, and the special object **[]**.

Words are used to name objects, and represent many kinds of thing – including English words. Their main features are that they consist of a sequence of characters, and they may have a value (in which case the word is the name of a variable). Unlike lists, words are always kept unique, so that if two words are equal, they are also identical.

Numbers are used for the usual purposes. Most POP-11 implementations have several different number representations. Usually, this includes integers (whole numbers), and floating point numbers (decimals). Some implementations may also have different accuracies of these, such as 'double decimals', which are kept to a much higher precision; and 'bignums', which are whole numbers which can be any number of digits long. Your implementation may also have other types, such as rationals (fractions) and complex numbers (for mathematicians and engineers). These too might come in various flavours. Usually only the small integers and the smaller accuracy floating point numbers are simple objects, so equality is different to identity.

Booleans are used to represent truth and falsity. They are unique objects, and you can't make any more of them. Indeed, the whole logic behind them requires that there are exactly two of them. All the conditional operations which test for truth actually only test against <**false**>, and consider any other object to indicate truth. Each of the booleans is only equal to itself, and is therefore always identical too.

Procedures are the actions of POP-11. They come ready-made, as built in procedures, or you can define your own. Procedures contain lots of information which constitutes their actions, but this is usually in a form which is inaccessible to you. However, you can find out a few things about them, like how many arguments they were declared to have, and so on. Two procedures are equal if your system can tell that they would do the same thing – normally this means that they are identical. It all depends on what information your system can find out about the procedures.

Vectors look very much like lists, but their internal representation is quite different. They are also used to clump objects together, and can have any objects in them. They are most useful where you have a fixed number of things in a collection, and won't want to change it. But finding a particular numbered element is very quick. Vectors do not have heads or tails like lists, and most procedures for manipulating lists don't work on vectors. Vectors are made whenever needed, and so are normally not identical when they are equal.

References are very simple: they are single-element records, a bit like half a pair, or a single-element list. They find their main application in exactly the kind of program you have been warned against at the end of the section on lists. Refs are made whenever needed, and so are normally not identical when they are equal.

Strings are sequences of characters, and are used for representing text and printing messages. They are unlike words in that they don't have values, aren't names of variables, and don't have any rules about what characters can follow which others. They are made whenever needed, and equality is not identity.

Arrays are used to collect up a group of objects, where you want to access them by numbers. They come in different dimensions (the number of numbers to get a particular object) and are often used to represent pictures, matrices, and tables of objects. Equal arrays might not be identical.

Properties are used to make 'lookup tables', which associate a value against an object.

Termin is a special unique object, which is used to represent the 'end' of something; for example, the end of a file. It is only equal to itself.

Keys are special objects which are used to represent the type of an object. Keys are at the root of POP-11, and the next chapter is devoted to them.

User-defined types. POP-11 lets you define your own data types. These come in two classes; 'record' and 'vector'. The record class objects always have the same number of objects in them, while vector class objects can vary in length.

Procedures for All Types

Some procedures will work on any object. For example, it is possible to compare any two objects for equality. There are other procedures which give useful information about any object for which they make sense.

For structures which can contain other objects, there are a few procedures which give information about the contents. Special interpretations are given under the section on the data type.

A new notation is used to describe procedures. In it, a word shown like this: *OBJECT* stands for any expression which produces a given kind of thing. In this example, it could be any object at all, perhaps the number 1234 or an expression which returns a word, like hd([hello there]). After an assignment arrow, a word such as *LENGTH* stands for the result of the procedure, and could be assigned into a variable, or used as part of a more complicated expression.

length(*OBJECT*) -> *LENGTH*;
> Gives the number of things contained in the object. Numbers do not have lengths, nor do ordinary procedures.

explode(*OBJECT*) -> *CONTENTS*;
> Stacks all the objects in the object. The number of things stacked will be the same as the length of the object.

datalist(*OBJECT*) -> *LIST*;
> Returns a list of all the things in the object. The length of the list will be the same as the length of the object.

dataword(*OBJECT*) -> *DWORD*;
> Returns a word indicating the type of the argument. For example, the dataword of a procedure is the word procedure.

datakey(*OBJECT*) -> *KEY*;
> Returns the key of the argument, which indicates what type of object it is. See Chapter 9.

copy(*OBJECT*) -> *COPY*:
> Returns a copy of the argument. The copy will be equal to the argument, but not identical. This procedure may not make sense on some data types. This is a top level copy only; the elements of the copy will be identical to the elements of the argument.

Character Codes

Every computer system must have some way of representing characters: the letters, digits and symbols of the language. POP-11 does this by using numbers for the characters. These are of use when manipulating POP-11 words, for strings and for when you need things to be printed in a special way on your screen or printer.

In choosing a cypher like this, there are two main questions: how many different symbols will there be, and which numbers represent which characters. The cohering features amongst the most-used codes are that the size of the code is a power of two, and that published standards are weaker than companies' ideas.

On all current POP-11 systems, the standard is called ASCII, which stands for

American Standard Code for Information Interchange, and has been adopted, with modifications, as an international standard. There are several versions of the standard: the predominant one has 128 symbols in it, of which 95 are 'graphic' symbols such as letters, digits, and symbols. The other 33 have various meanings, which depend mainly on your computer system. The standard also has national variants, where some of the 95 graphic symbols are needed for the particular country: for example the number 92 represents \ in England, ç in France, and ö in Germany.

Your system will almost certainly use either British or American ASCII, as the others have no square brackets. A further complication: characters are stored in at least eight bits on POP-11 systems. This allows 256 characters, of which 128 will be as described above, and the other 128 could be anything. IBM personal computers have a sensible assignment for the other 128, which gives circumflexes, umlauts, and other symbols of national importance. In this scheme, the 95 graphic codes are as per the United States, and the 'top 128' codes have things like pictures of people smiling, crosses and lines for drawing forms, as well as French, German and other characters. For example, \ is 92, ç is 135, and ö is 148. Apple Macintosh computers also have a scheme like this.

In ASCII, the codes which aren't graphic are 'control codes', so called because they are for controlling the display device, or whatever they are being sent to. Of these, a few have special significance. They are the linefeed, the tab, the return, and the formfeed. The main problem is that few computer systems use them in the same way.

Roughly speaking:

tab   means move right to the next tab stop, which is usually every eight columns. But sometimes it is every four, and sometimes it is something else. (ASCII code 9)

linefeed means go down a line. Sometimes you end up in the left margin, sometimes you just move straight down one line. (ASCII code 10)

return   means move to the left margin, and sometimes moving down a line too. (ASCII code 13)

formfeed means (when printing on paper) go to the top of the next page. Sometimes it clears the screen on VDUs. (ASCII code 12)

In POP-11, you can regard the linefeed code (10) as a 'newline' character, which is what it is usually called. This moves you to the start of the next line. Of course, the final arbiter will be your implementors and your computer system.

Finally, there are other standards than ASCII, and your machine may use one of those. For example, some IBM computers use a standard called EBCDIC, which is an 8-bit code.

Type by Type

This section covers details of each of the types, and introduces any special procedures for manipulating them.

Words

Words are one of the most important data types. They are used extensively within the system, and within almost every program. They are always kept unique, so any two words which have the same characters in them will be the same word. This is useful for use with properties.

The recogniser:

isword(*ITEM*) -> *BOOL*;
Returns a boolean value indicating if the argument is a word.

There are several ways to make words: although they are almost always made at the time your program is read in by POP-11. The simplest way to get hold of a particular word as a data object is the 'quoted word' mechanism. In this, you merely list the characters of the word between double-quote marks. However, there are rules for quoted words. Roughly speaking, the rules are used to separate words on sensible boundaries. For example, the rules say you can't put parentheses in your words. They also say you can't put single quote marks, which can be a problem if you need apostrophes for some reason. The full rules are as follows.

Characters each belong to a 'character class'. The exact classes depend somewhat on your system, but these rules will work on any.

Alphabetic:	a ... z, A ...Z
Digit:	0 1 2 3 4 5 6 7 8 9
Sign:	! # $ & | ˉ * - + / : < = > @ ˆ ?
Separator:	; " % ( ) [ ] { } , .
String Quote:	'
Character Quote:	'
Underscore:	_
Backslash:	/

Systems which have special character sets which include other symbols may have rules for those symbols too. Typically, letters with accents will be alphabetic, and other symbols will be sign characters.

A quoted word consists of:
An alphabetic character, followed by any sequence of alphabetic and digit characters, or

Any sequence of sign characters, or

A single separator, string quote or character quote character, or

Any word from the rules above, preceded or followed by any number of underscore characters, or

Any number of words from the rules above, with underscore characters in between.

The exact handling of the backslash character may differ, but normally it will be considered a sign character. You may find that it is an 'alphabeticiser' character, which makes the following character be considered (temporarily) an alphabetic character.

Note that upper and lower case letters are considered different.

If for some reason you need to make a word which won't obey the rules for quoted words, you can make a string, and use the procedure consword:

consword(*STRING*) -> *WORD*;
> Returns a word which has the same characters as the string. Any character sequence is allowed.

Words may be subscripted:

word(*INTEGER*) -> *CHAR*;
> Returns a character from the word. For example, subscripting the word hello by 3 gives the number which represents the character l. The first character has subscript 1.

subscrw(*INTEGER, WORD*) -> *CHAR*;
> Behaves exactly like the subscripting using the brackets. Of the two, this is the more primitive method: the first is just a shorthand for using subscrw.

Words are also the names of variables. It is sometimes useful to be able to get at the value of a variable whose name you have.

valof(*WORD*) -> *VALUE*;
> Returns the value of the variable whose name is the argument word. The value is the current environment's value (see section on dynamic scoping). This procedure may cause the system to declare the variable, and may cause autoloading. This procedure has an updater.

You can find out if a word is the name of a variable. Every variable has a syntactic class, known as its 'identifier properties', or identprops.

identprops(*WORD*) -> *IDENT*;
> Returns the identifier properties of the argument word, which indicates the syntactic properties of the word. Words which aren't the names of variables

have the word **undef** as their identprops, ordinary variables have the value O. Other types are described in the section on procedures.

Notes on general procedures: the **length** of a word is the number of characters in the word. The **datalist** of a word is a list of all the characters in the word, represented as numbers appropriate to the host system: see section on character codes.

Lists

Lists are the most ubiquitous data type, yet aren't actually a primitive type of POP-11. They are constructed as a chain of pairs, together with the special object []. Their characteristic is a linked chain of pointers to objects.

They are formed from their special syntax using square brackets. Inside a list, words do not represent variable references; instead, they are simply words. To take the value of a variable, precede its name by an up-arrow. If the word names a variable which contains a list, you may precede the name by a double up-arrow, which will insert all the elements of the named variable's list into the present one. To construct a list by evaluating some code, surround the code with percent signs. The following equality test shows the equivalence of up-arrow and percent notation:

```
: vars x;
: [hello there] -> x;
: [`x ``x] = [% x, explode(x) %] =>
** <true>
```

Recogniser:

islist(*ITEM*) -> *BOOL*;

Returns a boolean result indicating if the argument is a list. For the purposes of this procedure, a list is defined to be either [], or a pair whose back is a pair or [], or a dynamic list (described later).

Lists are only copied where necessary. This means that some lists share tail sections. The primitive list operations are shown here:

OBJECT :: *LIST* -> *RESULT*;

Returns a list one longer than the second argument. The head of the result is the *OBJECT*. *LIST* is not copied in this procedure: therefore, the tail of the result is identical to the second argument. This procedure mishaps if the second argument is not a list.

hd(*LIST*) ->*RESULT*;
Returns the head of the list. This procedure mishaps if the argument has no head; it must be a list with at least one element in it.

tl(*LIST*) -> *RESULT*;
Returns the tail of the list. This procedure mishaps if the argument has no tail; it must be a list with at least one element in it, that is, not **[]**.

These last two procedures have updaters:

NEW -> **hd**(*LIST*);
NEW -> (*LIST*);
Changes the head/tail of the list to be the new object. These procedures mishap if list is not a list with at least one element; the updater of **tl** mishaps if *NEW* is not a list. These procedures are known as 'list surgery', and can be very dangerous.

Lists may be subscripted:

LIST(*INTEGER*) -> *ELEMENT*;
Returns an element of the list. Subscripting by 1 is the same as taking the head of a list. Subscripts must be from 1 to the length of the list, or this will generate a mishap.

subscrl(*INTEGER*, *LIST*) -> *ELEMENT*;
Behaves just like the subscripting using the brackets. The former method is just a shorthand for using **subscrl**.

LEFT <> *RIGHT* -> *NEW*;
Returns a new list whose length is the sum of the lengths of its two arguments. The new list consists of the elements of *LEFT* followed by the elements of *RIGHT*. The *RIGHT* list is not copied; therefore by taking subsequent tails of *NEW* you will eventually find a list identical to *RIGHT*. This procedure actually works with arguments of any type, so long as *LEFT* and *RIGHT* are of the same type. *NEW* will be a longer object of the same type as the arguments.

Pairs are primitive data objects. Each pair contains exactly two objects. When built by the system in list manipulations, the backs of pairs only ever point to lists (as defined under **islist**, above).
Recogniser:
ispair(*ITEM*) -> *BOOL*;
Returns a boolean indicating if the argument is a pair.

Constructor:
conspair(*F*, *B*) -> *PAIR*;
Returns a new pair, whose front is the first argument, and whose back is the second argument. This is similar to the list cons procedure ::, except that the second

argument may be any object, rather than being restricted to being a list.

Access:

front(*PAIR*) -> *ITEM*;
back(*PAIR*) -> *ITEM*;

These procedures return the front or back of a pair. They are very similiar to **hd** and **tl**, except that they don't check that the object is a list: they check that it is a pair. Compare **ispair** and **islist** for the difference. Note that **[]** is not a pair. **front** and **back** both have updaters.

A complication to lists is the dynamic list. This is a very useful data type, constructed out of procedures and pairs. A dynamic list behaves just like an ordinary list, except when printing, when it may have ellipsis just before the closing bracket. It has an 'expanded length', which is the number of items known to be in the list.

Constructor:

pdtolist(*PDR*) -> *DLIST*;

Returns a dynamic list, of expanded length 0, from the given procedure. **pdtolist** mishaps if its argument is not a procedure. The procedure should take no arguments.

Example:

```
: vars n;
: 0 -> n;

: define nextnum();
:    n + 1 -> n;
:    n;
: enddefine;

: vars dlist;
: pdtolist(nextnum) -> dlist;
: dlist =>
** [...]
: dlist(5) =>
** 5
: dlist =>
** [1 2 3 4 5 ...]
```

Initially the dynamic list contains no known elements: it has not been expanded. Whenever a list procedure requires an element, it is computed by using the procedure the list was made from. This is useful for making infinite lists (for example, a list of all the prime numbers), or for making queues (the procedure fetches objects in, and conventional list processing removes them from the left end). If the procedure returns the special object **termin**, then the list is closed, and the procedure won't be called upon to provide more elements; and it will no longer print with ellipsis. A dynamic list with no elements in it is equal to the special object **[]**, but may not be identical to it.

It is possible to have a list of POP-11 code, and execute it:

popval(*LIST*):

Executes the code given in the list, in the current environment. This is useful if your program writes and runs its own programs. Any results of the code in the list are left on the stack.

Example:

```
: vars x;
: [] -> x;
: x =>
** []
: popval([3 -> x;]);
: x =>
** 3
```

Numbers

It has been said that the 'natural' numbers (1, 2, 3 ...) are god-given, and all else is the work of man. Arithmetic has been with us a long time, and over the years the mathematicians have done much work. The main historical trend has been to try various operations on them and see what you get. So if you start subtracting bigger numbers from smaller ones you get zero and negative numbers: now we have 'integers' (... –2, –1, 0, 1, 2 ...). If you divide integers that 'don't go' you get fractions, such as 2/3: the 'rationals'. When you start taking square roots you can get 'irrational' numbers. If you take square roots of negative numbers you get 'imaginary' numbers.

So, the mathematicians have found many different classifications of numbers. Other people have more restricted tastes: typically when you count things, you use integers. When you measure things you use decimals (a particular bunch of rational numbers), and complex numbers are mostly used by scientists and engineers.

Numeric computation is a subject which has been investigated at great length; suffice to say that most computer scientists have views on the subject. From a computing standpoint, the main interest has been in representation: how should a number of a particular kind be represented in a machine, and how can useful operations be performed on that representation. Typically, programming systems would just deal with some rational numbers, represented in binary.

In POP-11, the bias has always been to make numeric computations make sense from a mathematically naive standpoint. What follows is a discussion of various kinds of numbers which POP-11 systems have. Note though that not all systems have the same kinds of numbers, and the ones which they all have are not necessarily done in the same way. You will have to consult your system documentation for further detailed information.

However, there are some basic concepts which you should be familiar with, as they have impact on a great many programs.

As you know, conventional computers are binary creatures, and any particular computer has a characteristic word* size. This is, roughly speaking, the size of the biggest objects which it can manipulate easily; usually it is some even power of two. On most of the machines which POP-11 runs on, the word size is 32 bits, which is to say that a word consists of 32 ones or zeros in a row. Of course, any interpretation can be put on these patterns, but for the present section we are interested in numeric interpretations.

With a 32-bit word, there are 2^{32} different patterns. Usually, these would be used to represent the integers (whole numbers) -2^{31} to $2^{31}-1$ ($-2,147,483,648$ to $2,147,483,647$). Another scheme is to break the 32 bits into two parts, say 20 bits and 12 bits, and use these to represent the two numbers which form a floating point number.

However, POP-11 systems, like many LISP and PROLOG systems, need to be able to distinguish simple objects such as these integers, from pointers to structures – that is, addresses. (See the section at the beginning of this chapter.) Often this is done by saying that all integers will have some particular pattern in a few of the bits. This reduces the number of bits available to represent the integers, say down to 30 bits. In POPLOG, the system uses two bits to tag whether the object is a simple or not; and the two tag bits also say if the object is an integer or a floating point number.

POP-11 always converts numbers from one type to another as appropriate – decided by the implementors of your system. Unless you are especially concerned with numeric processing you shouldn't have to worry about this, although it is a good idea to find out at least how the different types print on your system. This way you can recognise them if they crop up, which might indicate a bug in your program. (For example, you might take square roots of negative numbers by mistake, and end up with complex numbers.)

Integers. All POP-11 implementations have integers, as simple objects. The range of values for integers is system dependent, but see note under Bigints, below. These are the basic whole numbers, and include zero and negative numbers.

Floating Point. All POP-11 implementations have floating point numbers, usually as simple objects. The range of values is system dependent.

As with other modern languages for artificial intelligence, POP-11 systems tend to have other forms of number as well. These are normally structures which live in memory, as they may have to be bigger than can fit in a single word.

Bigint. A 'bigint', or big integer is a whole number which needs more space than fits

---

* This use of 'word' is entirely unrelated to the POP-11 data structure 'word'; it is the conventional, if unfortunate, term.

in the word size of the host computer. The idea is that you can represent any whole number with perfect accuracy. These can be slow if you do a lot of calculation with them. Most current implementations of POP-11 have bigints (in common with LISP systems). Between these and the simple integers, your system ought to be able to represent numbers up to at least 24 bits (–8,388, 608 to 8,388, 607).

Higher Precision Floats. The floating point theme has some variations. These are normally represented as $a\ 2^b$, where a is called the *mantissa*, and b the *exponent*. Mathematically, this is similar to the $x \S 10^y$ often found on calculators, and known as 'scientific notation'. The problem with this is that we are restricted in the values we can give to a because we only have (say) 20 bits to express it in, which is about six significant decimal digits, thus limiting the accuracy of the number. Also, we only have (say) 12 bits for the exponent, which limits the magnitude of the number. So, most computer systems have several accuracies of floating point number, for different purposes, and so does at least one implementation of POP-11. You will have to check your system documentation for the details of what you have. The representations with higher accuracy are also slower in calculations, and take more space.

Rationals. Following on from bignums are rational numbers. These are fractions, and are actually represented in POP-11 as $p\ /\ q$, where p and q would normally be bignums. Rationals let you have unlimited accuracy, although clearly they can cost unlimited computing power to work with.

Complex. For mathematicians and engineers, at least one implementation of POP-11 has complex numbers. These are numbers which have two parts, an imaginary and a real, usually represented in the form $x + iy$, where x and y are ordinary numbers, and i is the square root of –1. The real part is x, and the imaginary part is iy. Given that complex numbers are formed from two 'ordinary' numbers, there are a number of options. The implementation which has complex numbers, POPLOG, has two forms; one built from rationals, the other from floating point numbers.

Recognisers: all the forms of number available to you will have recogniser procedures, called **isX**, where **X** is the name of the type as defined in your documentation. There is also a generic **isnumber**, for recognising any form of number, and a few special recognisers for grouping the different forms together.

isnumber(*ITEM*) -> *BOOL*;
    Returns a boolean indicating if the argument was a number of any description.

isintegral(*ITEM*) -> *BOOL*;
    Returns a boolean indicating if the argument was of a'whole number' type; either a simple integer or a big integer.

Numeric Procedures

Without functions to manipulate them, numbers are of no use. POP-11 has the usual gang of arithmetic procedures, plus a few unusual ones. The exact set of functions is dependent on what kinds of number your system has, and what your implementors decided was useful.

$A + B \to C$;	addition
$A - B \to C$;	subtraction
$A * B \to C$;	multiplication
$A / B \to C$;	division
$A ** B \to C$;	exponentiation
$-A \to C$;	negation
negate(A)	
abs(A) ->	
max(A, B)	
min(A, B)	
sign(A) -> C;	give sign multiplier
random(A) -> C;	give random integer

Each takes arguments as shown, and produces a single result. Exponentiation is the process of multiplying A by itself B times. Both $-A$ and negate(A) return the same result. The absolute value of a number is found by ignoring any minus sign it may have. The 'bigger' number chosen by max is the most positive of the two arguments; min picks the most negative. The 'sign multiplier' of a number is one of $-1, +1$, and 0: sign(A) * abs(A) is always the number you first thought of. The random integer returned by random is always between 1 and the argument, inclusive.

A div $B \to C$;	take quotient
A mod $B \to C$;	take remainder

The two procedures div and mod only work when their arguments are integral: div returns the number of times B goes into A, as a whole number; mod returns the remainder after dividing A by B. If your system only has integral numbers, / will be the same as div. mod always returns a number whose absolute value (ignore any minus signs) is less than the absolute value of B: but be warned that this may be negative.

fracof(A) -> B;	take fractional part
intof(A) -> B;	take integer part
round(A) -> B;	round to nearest integer

Systems which have floating point numbers also have these functions. Note that intof and round actually return integral type results if possible. Note also that round is defined as intof(A + 0.5), which may not be appropriate for sophisticated statistical processing.

sin(A) -> B;	trigonometric functions
cos(A) -> B;	
tan(A) -> B;	
arcsin(A) -> B;	inverse trigonometric functions
arccos(A) -> B;	
arctan(A) -> B;	
arctan2(X, Y) -> A;	inverse of **tan**, gives quadrant
pi =>	useful constant
popradians =>	control variable

Systems which support floating point numbers also have this set of trigonometric functions. The first three take an angle and return a value; the next three are the inverse of the first. **arctan2** gives the arc tangent of X/Y, giving the correct quadrant. There is a system variable called **popradians**, which controls the units of the arguments. If this variable has the value <false>, then the arguments are assumed to be in degrees, where sin(90) returns 1. Otherwise, the units are assumed to be in radians, where sin(pi / 2) returns 1. The default is <false>, that is, it assumes degrees. The ranges (allowable arguments) of the functions are dependent on your system, as is the accuracy of the results. Systems which have complex numbers support them in these functions. Your system may also have other similar functions, such as hyperbolic trigonometric functions.

exp(A) -> B;	exponential
log(A) -> B;	natural logarithm
sqrt(A) -> B;	square root

Systems which have floating point numbers also have these functions. The exponential of a number is the number e raised to the power of the number. (e is a mathematical magic number which crops up all over the place, and has a value which is approximately 2.718. Like pi, the digits go on forever.) The natural logarithm of a number works exactly like a conventional 'common' logarithm (to base 10), but the resulting numbers are bigger: it is defined as the power which e has to be raised to to get your number. You use **exp** to find antilogarithms. Natural logarithms are also called Naperian logarithms, after the Scottish mathematician John Napier, who was born in 1550 and some say invented the decimal point. The function **sqrt** returns the square root of a number. These functions work with complex numbers on the systems which support those.

Booleans

You have already met the boolean objects <true> and <false>. This section is the final word on them.

There are exactly two of these objects, and they are represented as unique objects, normally as structures in memory. They print as they are named, with angle brackets around them.

There is no special syntax for writing them; instead, there are two constants named true and false, whose values are the boolean objects. This book has adopted the convention of referring to them by their printed notation, as that is how you would first see them, but if you ever need to refer to one, you refer to it via its constant:

: true =>
** <true>

As described in the chapter on conditional expressions, all built in conditional tests actually test against <false>, and consider any other value to represent truth. As such, many procedures will return an 'answer', or <false> to indicate that they were unable to produce an answer. The procedure issubstring is an example, in the section on strings below.

Recogniser:

isboolean(*ITEM*) -> *BOOL*;
Returns a boolean indicating if the argument was a boolean. That is, if the argument was the object <false> or the object <true>, the result will be <true>. Otherwise, the result is <false>, as there are only two boolean objects.

Procedures

From many perspectives, the procedure is easily the most complicated of all the POP-11 structures, and has the most details to explain. Because of this, procedures have several chapters to themselves in this book. Most of the procedures which work on procedures are described in the other chapters, as they are inappropriate without an understanding of the variations of procedure. However, this section is concerned with procedures as data objects, as they have some aspects in common with all data objects.

One of the special features of POP-11 is that procedures are first class data objects, unlike in most other languages, including most versions of LISP. This means that they can be passed as arguments to other procedures, returned as results, stored in variables, and placed inside other structures such as lists, without any special syntax or work.

Procedures as Arguments: To exemplify this, we introduce the procedure maplist, which requires that one of its arguments is a procedure.

maplist(*LIST, PDR*) -> *LIST*;

Applies the argument procedure to each element of the argument list, and returns a list of all the results.

So, if we had a list of objects, and wanted to find a list of all the lengths of those objects, we could simply do:

```
: maplist([[] [uno] [un deux] [h e l l o]], length) =>
** [0 1 2 5]
```

As you see, no special syntax is needed to pass the procedure length as an argument. The reason for this is that length is an ordinary identifier whose value is a procedure. When POP-11 ran the example above, it made the call to maplist without knowing what kind of object the value of length was: it just pushed it in the normal way.

It should be mentioned that this is one of POP-11's most powerful features, and is one of the prime benefits of weak typing. It means that not only can we write procedures which operate on many different data structures (because we don't have to say what type the arguments are), we can also supply arbitrary procedures to do the work, as we can pass procedures in as arguments. It must be said that many other languages allow you to do this too, although not as simply as this.

Here's a definition of a trivial procedure which takes a procedure as argument, and applies it to the word hello to see what happens:

```
define testonhello(pdr);
    pdr("hello");
enddefine;
```

As you see, no special syntax is needed here either. Try this procedure, passing in isword and length.

Procedures as Results: From the simplicity with which you can pass procedures into other procedures, you will not be suprised at how easy it is to pass them out too. A simple example should tell you all you need to know; so here's a trivial (and silly) procedure which returns a boolean-returning or number-returning procedure.

```
define boolornum(w);
vars w;
    if w = "bool" then
        isword;
    else
        length;
    endif;
enddefine;
```

Procedures in Variables and Structures: The ideas shown above should give you the picture that anything you can do with ordinary objects you can do with procedures. However, as this is unusual in programming languages, it is worthwhile being explicit about them.

You may assign procedures into variables:

```
: vars mylength;
: length -> mylength;
: mylength("four") =>
** 4
```

You can print procedures, but this takes a little explanation. In common with other data types for which there is no natural printing method, POP-11 prints procedures by printing the name of the type in angle brackets. Unknown to you, all the built-in procedures, and those you define with the **define** keyword, have a name attached to them, known as the **pdprops**. Procedures retain their **pdprops**, as it is part of their structure. So the procedure in the variable **mylength**, above, retains the **pdprops** of **length**, even when assigned into the variable **mylength**:

```
: mylength =>
** <procedure length>
```

You may put procedures into structures. A classical use for this is to provide a method of tying actions to data objects, which can be phenomenally useful.

Here a list with a procedure in it:

```
: [^mylength] =>
** [<procedure length>]
```

Finally, a more sophisticated example. The procedure we'll define as **eval** is most of the workings of a LISP interpreter. This uses a structure which consists of a list of two-element lists. Each of the sublists has two procedures in it. The leftmost one is an applicability test, and the one on the right is the action.

First, some notes on some procedures: **identfn** is a procedure which does absolutely nothing, and here it is behaving as a procedure which returns its argument unmodified; **valof** is a procedure which takes a word and returns its value (see section on words above); **apply** takes a single argument which should be a procedure, which it calls. And one more:

```
define dolist(list);
    explode(tl(list));
    eval(hd(list));
enddefine;
```

Now, the structure:

```
: vars actions;
: [[^isnumber ^identfn]
: [^isword ^valof]
: [^isprocedure ^apply]
: [^islist ^dolist]] -> actions;
```

What can we do with this? Well, here's a procedure which uses it:

```
define eval(item);
vars testaction test action;
    for testaction in actions do
        testaction(1) -> test;
        testaction(2) -> action;
        if test(item) then
            return(action(item));
        endif;
    endfor;
    [i am a failure]
enddefine;
```

(A note on style: returning the failure list is an apology for an error handler. What you should do here depends on your application. A real system would make a mishap.)

This style of programming is known as *data driven*, as it is the structure of the data (the list **actions**) which does all the work, although people sometimes argue about whether procedures in lists count as data or procedures. A compromise answer is that, in POP-11, they can be both.

It is a good exercise to work through **eval** and decide why it behaves the same as the following **eval2**. You might also like to think about which you consider to be better style: which has more structure? Who provides the structure? Which is easier to read? Which is easier to debug? Which is more powerful? Could a program write both of these procedures? Modify them?

```
define eval2(item);
    if isnumber(item) then
        item;
    elseif isword(item) then
        valof(item);
    elseif isprocedure(item) then
        item();
    elseif islist(item) then
        explode(tl(item));
        eval2(hd(item));
    else
        [i am a failure]
    endif;
enddefine;
```

Recogniser:

isprocedure(*ITEM*) -> *BOOL*;
Returns a boolean indicating if the argument is a procedure.

As procedures are so versatile, they are often used to implement other structures which would normally be thought of as data structures. For example, at least one implementation of POP-11 uses procedures to implement arrays.

CHAPTER 9

Class Procedures and Keys

Introduction

Few languages have such a clear definition of what constitutes their data types as POP-11. Each data type, or class, has well-defined attributes, and the central unifying concept is the key.

The Need for Keys

As summarised in the preceding chapter, the basic operations on the data objects are common to every type. Let's take printing as an example. You will have seen that you can print out (on your screen) any POP-11 object, normally using the printarrow. The printarrow causes various procedures to be run, for example to print the ** and so on. It uses a procedure called pr to actually print each object on the stack.

Now, it would be perfectly possible to write pr in such a way as it knew about every data class in POP-11. But what would be better is to have one procedure for each class, whose sole job was to print out objects for one class. More than this: it would be responsible for all the printing of objects of that class.

The job for pr is now much simpler: all it has to do to print a given object is find out what class it belongs to, and then call the appropriate printing procedure on it.

Now the only procedure which absolutely must be able to work on any object is the procedure for discovering the class of an object. The mechanism is simple: each class is represented by an object called its key. And every object has a reference to its key; just as if each person had their nationality stamped on their forehead. So if we take the key of any word, we get the word key; the key of every procedure is the procedure key. Keep in mind that the key is not of the same class as the class it represents. It is more like a mascot, perhaps a teddy bear. The teddy bear represents a school of children, not teddy bears. Keep this in mind if you get confused by the terminology:

mascot   =   key
school   =   data class
children =   the data objects
lessons =   procedures applicable to data objects

All we need is a method for getting the printing procedure for a particular class,

118

given that we now have an object which represents the class. But this procedure is simple, as all it has to know about are keys.

The details of what the primitive procedures are are not what is important, and are somewhat system-dependent. What is important is to understand that the generic procedures always delegate to specialist procedures for each class. These are termed, for example, the 'class printing' procedure, and the 'class equals' procedure, and so on.

This mechanism is better for several reasons. In implementation terms, the work a class printing procedure does is more closely related to the class equals of the same class than to the class printer for a different class. Also, because there is a uniform method for getting to the class printing procedures, adding a new class, or redefining a class printer becomes simpler.

There are conceptual benefits too. You will remember that if **x** is a list,

: x(3) =>

will print the third element of the list. But if **x** is a procedure, then the same expression will push 3 and then apply **x**. What happens here is that the 'application brackets' really mean run the class apply procedure of the class of the object. The class apply for lists is a procedure which finds the *n*th element, while the class apply for procedures simply invokes them. Further, you will probably have found out that if **x** was a boolean, you will get a mishap. Representing this with the class scheme is simple: the class apply for booleans is a procedure which causes a mishap.

There is a procedure for finding the key of any object (**datakey**), and for each primitive operation there is a procedure for finding the specialist procedure for that operation (for example **class _ print** and **class _ apply**). In fact, there are also identifiers for each key: their names are formed from the name of the class, with _**key** appended. So you can try:

: word _ key =>
** <key word>

Imagine a grid with the data classes along one side, and all the primitive operations along the other. In a POP-11 system, every single one of those procedures exists. Many of them will be the values of variables, and have familiar names such as **consword**. But we can get to all of them by using **datakey** and, for example, **class _ cons**. Do remember, however, that many of these operations don't actually make sense, and so their procedures simply cause mishaps. For example, the system won't let you build another boolean object. The point, however, is that if you wanted to do it, the expression you would have to write is defined.

To make this discussion concrete, consider the printing example again. The procedure **pr** functions as though it was defined like this:

```
define pr(item);
vars key specialist;
    datakey(item) -> key;
    class_print(key) -> specialist;
    specialist(item);
enddefine;
```

Or, more concisely:

```
define pr(item);
    class_print(datakey(item))(item);
enddefine;
```

So, for the example of building another boolean object, the expression is

```
class_cons(boolean_key)();
```

This expression will mishap: but to state it again, the point here is that if the operation was sensible, the expression would work.

Fixed Size and Variable Size Classes

We have met the distinction between simple and compound data objects previously. If it still a little hazy, just remember that only numbers can be simple.

Of the compound objects, we can make another broad distinction. This is to do with how many fields objects of a given class can have: a vector can be of any length while a pair has exactly two fields, the front and the back.

There are a number of special objects which have no fields, but are nonetheless compound: this is just a special case of a fixed number of fields. Fixed at zero.

So, there are two categories: vector category, which has a variable number of fields; and record category, where it is fixed. The fundamental difference between the two is that a size must be stored for each individual object of a vector category class, while we only need to store the size once for a record category class.

Because of this difference, getting hold of the innards is different between the two categories. Record category classes have one procedure for each field, for example pairs have the procedures **front** and **back**. Vector category classes have a single procedure for accessing any field, but the procedure takes a number to say which field is wanted. Words, for example, can have different numbers of characters, and so are vector category. So there is the single procedure **subscrw** for getting at the fields, which takes a number to say which one you want. See the preceding chapter for descriptions of **front, back** and **subscrw**.

Size of a Field

Almost without exception, any POP-11 object which has fields can put any object in those fields. Now for the exceptions: strings and words. The only thing which can be put in these are characters, which are represented as numbers.

Every field has a specifier, which describes what can be put into it. The exact field specifiers available differ from implementation to implementation, but there are two basic types: full fields and restricted fields. A full field is represented by the word full, while restricted fields are represented by either integers or some other word.

You can put any object into a full field: these are the only kind we have really covered so far. All the fields in pairs and vectors and so on are full.

The only common place where there are restricted fields are the fields for characters in strings and words. Their values are restricted to be integers in a given range. For example, characters are usually eight bits long, so their field specifier is the integer 8. If the specifier is positive, it means that the values in the field are regarded as unsigned. In this case, it means they go from 0 to 2^8-1 (which is 255) inclusive. If the specifier is negative, the values are regarded as signed, in which case they would go from -2^{8-1} to $2^{8-1}-1$, which is -128 to 127, inclusive.

Summary of field specifiers:

The word full: Any POP-11 object.
Positive integer n: Any integer in the range 0 to 2^n.
Negative integer n: Any integer in the range -2^{n-1} to $2^{n-1}-1$.

These are covered in more detail in the next chapter, in the section on making your own data classes with **vectorclass** and **recordclass**.

Keys as Data Objects

Keys are proper first-class data objects in their own right, and so you can pass them around in the normal ways, put them in structures, and so on.

You can *always* find the key of *any* object, and compare keys in the normal ways: it is the primitive method of finding out what type an object is. Keys print in default format, with the dataword of the type, like this:

```
: datakey("hello") =>
** <key word>
```

In fact, it is more than the primitive method of discovering a data type of an object, it is the definition. Every object in the memory of the computer has a (so far) secret mark on it, which is a pointer to a key. This is literally the essence of being of a given class. You get at the secret mark with **datakey**.

There is no way to change the key of an object: you can't do this:

```
: pair_key -> datakey("hello");
```

When people talk about converting things from one class to another, what they actually mean is building another object which somehow corresponds to the original. They never mean that you actually change the original object.

All the recogniser procedures are written in terms of keys. So, for example, the procedure **isword** could have been written like this:

```
define isword(item);
    datakey(item) = datakey("anyword");
enddefine;
```

datakey(*ITEM*) -> *KEY*;
Returns the key of the argument.

This procedure lets you write an **issameclass** procedure, for finding out if any two objects are of the same class:

```
define issameclass(a, b);
    datakey(a) = datakey(b)
enddefine;
```

Rembering that every object effectively has a secret pointer to its key, and that the key contains procedures for the primitive actions, we can draw box diagrams for keys. Figure 9.1 shows a pair and the pair key. The top box of the pair is the secret reference to its key, while inside the pair key are some number of pointers to the procedures for the primitive actions. But where is the secret pointer of the key?

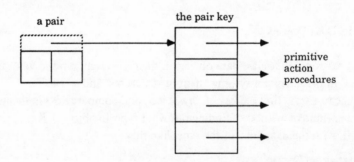

Fig. 9.1

Recogniser: Just like any other object, it is possible to recognise keys.

iskey(*ITEM*) -> *BOOL*;

Returns a boolean indicating if the argument was a key or not.

The Key is the Key Key

If you can take the key of any object, and keys are first-class objects like any other, then you can take the key of a key. What do you get?

The answer is confusion. It is easier when you try it. Here's an object:

```
: varsxxkxkk;
: "someword" -> x;
```

Take its key:

```
: datakey(x) -> xk;
: xk =>
** <key word>
```

And take the key of that:

```
: datakey(xk) -> xkk;
: xkk =>
** <key key>
```

What is the thing in the box? The answer is the key key. Keys are objects, of their own class. Every class has a key. Ergo, there is a key key.

You should be able to see that in this example. We could have put any object into **x**, and **xkk** would still be the key key: because **datakey**(...) is a key, and the key of any key is the key key.

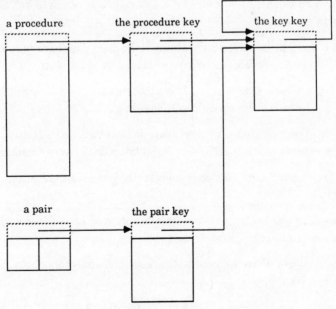

Fig. 9.2

It helps to have a diagram: Figure 9.2 shows a procedure, a pair, their keys, and the key key. It just shows the secret pointers to keys, not the contents of the procedure and the pair. You see that the key of the procedure is the procedure key, whose key is the key key. But the key of the pair is the pair key: the key of that is the key key again. And of course, the key of any key is the same. Take a deep breath: the key of the key key is the key key. Congratulations, you have reached the absolute centre of the POP-11 universe. The key key is only two pointers away from every other object in the POP-11 system.

Primitive Actions

The primitive actions which are defined for each class are these shown below. Notice that some of the actions don't make sense for all data classes. For example, what should construction do for integers?

Construction. For making a new object of the given class. You have to say what to put into the object. For vector categories, you also have to say how big to make it.

Initialisation. For vector category class objects only, there is a procedure which builds new, empty, objects of the given class. Empty means that you don't get to say what goes in it: it comes filled with some default values. Just regard it as a blank sheet. You just have to say how big to make it.

Destruction. You can get hold of all of the innards of any object in one go; and they all end up on the stack.

Recognition. You can recognise every object of the class. There is a procedure which can be applied to any object, and it says whether it is of the class.

Printing. You can print every object. The actual method for printing differs slightly for each class, as each class has different innards.

Specification. You can find out how many fields objects of the class have, and whether the number of fields is fixed or variable: record or vector category.

Accessing. For record category class objects only, you can get at or change the individual fields.

Subscripting. For vector category class objects only, you can subscript the object to get at the fields, or change them.

Application. You can write 'application brackets' and apply any object, in the same way as for procedures.

'Datawording'. Every class has a name (called the dataword), and you can find the name of the class of any object. Don't confuse the dataword with the key: in our

analogy, the key is the teddy bear, while its name is the name of the school, a word such as hollandpark or eton. The name of the pair class is the word pair.

Equality test. Every object can be compared for equality with any other, and there is a procedure for each class which knows how to perform the test.

Class Functions

There is a set of procedures to get from any key to the procedures which perform the primitive actions on the data objects. Each is named class_X, where X is the name of the primitive operation.

class_cons(*KEY*) -> *PDR*;

Returns the construction procedure for the class.

Vector Category. If the key is for a vector category type, then the procedure will require a number to say how big to make the new object, and what number of objects on the stack to put into the new object. Like this:

```
: class_cons(vector_key)("hello", "there", 2) =>
** {hello there}
```

This procedure is consvector, which constructs vectors. Also try consstring, which makes strings.

Record Category. If the key is for a record category class, then the procedure just requires the objects to make the new structure out of. Like this:

```
: class_cons(pair_key)("hello", []) =>
** [hello]
```

Remember that the list [hello] is made of a pair with the word in the front and the empty list in the back. This procedure is the same as conspair, which is the model for record category construction procedures.

class_init(*KEY*) -> *PDR*;

Returns the initialisation procedure for any vector category class: mishaps for record category classes. The initialiser is a procedure which takes a single argument, the number of fields for the structure to be made. This must be a integer zero or more:

```
: class_init(vector_key)(4) =>
**{undef undef undef undef}
```

The model procedures are initv and inits. These two names are anachronisms:

they should have been **initvector** and **initstring**. Structures which have full fields (the normal case) will be filled with the word **undef**. Structures which are restricted to numbers will have the value zero.

class_dest(*KEY*) -> *PDR*;

Returns the destructor procedure for the class.

Vector Category. If the key is of vector category class, the destruction procedure will stack all the elements of the object, followed by the number of elements:

```
: class_dest(vector_key)({hello there}) =>
** hello there 2
```

This is the same as the model procedure **destvector**. Notice that the results of the destructor match the arguments of the constructor. So you can do

```
: consv(destvector({hello there})) =>
** {hello there}
```
or
```
: class_cons(vector_key)
    (class_dest(vector_key)({hello})) =>
** {hello there}
```

Make sure you understand that a copy of the argument vector was made. It is not identical to the argument list.

Record Category. If the key is of record category class, the destruction procedure will simply stack the elements of the object, without the number of elements:

```
: class_dest(pair_key)([hello there]) =>
** hello [there]
```

This is the same as the model **destpair**.

Notice that like the vector version, the results of the destructor match the arguments of the constructor.

class_recognise(*KEY*) ->*PDR*;

Returns the recogniser procedure for the class. This is a procedure which may be applied to any object, and it returns a boolean indicating if the argument belongs to the class:

```
: class_recognise(word_key)([hello]) =>
** <false>
: class_recognise(word_key)("hello") =>
** <true>
```

This is the same as the model **isword**. All of the recognisers have their own names: **isprocedure**, **ispair** and so on.

class_print(*KEY*) -> *PDR*;

Returns the printing procedure for a given class. Of course, you can always print things with **pr**, which will call the appropriate class printer for you. The class printer is important because it has an updater, so you can change the way objects print.

  : class_print(integer_key)(34);
  34

Notice that it behaves just like **pr** would have done with the same argument, which is different from the printarrow, which prints stars and so on before calling **pr**.

Now suppose you had a procedure called **roman** which printed numbers in roman form: 34 would come out as **XXXIV**. To make the system use your printer, you do this:

  : roman -> class_print(integer_key);
  : 34 =>
  ** XXXIV

It is not recommended that you change the printing of built-in classes. This feature comes into its own for user-defined classes, described in the next chapter.

class_spec(*KEY*) -> *SPEC*;

Returns the specifier for the class. This tells you how many fields elements of the class have, and what their field specifiers are. The specifier for a record category is a list of field specifiers. The specifier for a vector category class is a single field specifier. See the section on field specifiers earlier in this chapter.

Special Case Categories. Classes which don't have fields (like integers and booleans) or whose insides aren't manipulable (like procedures) return <false> for their specifiers, rather than the [] you might expect. Examples of this include numbers and booleans:

  : class_spec(boolean_key) =>
  ** <false>

Vector Category. If the key is for a vector category type, the procedure will return a single field specifier, which will be a word or a number:

  : class_spec(vector_key) =>
  ** full

  : class_spec(string_key) =>
  ** 8

These two examples show that you can put any object into vectors, but only integers in the range 0 to 255 into strings.

Record Category. If the key is for a record category class, the procedure will return a list of field specifiers, one for each field of the record. For example,

```
: class_spec(pair_key) =>
** [full full]
: class_spec(ref_key) =>
** [full]
```

These show that pairs have two full fields, while references (presented in the following chapter) have just a single full field.

class_access(*N*, *KEY*) -> *PDR*;

Returns an accessing procedure for record category classes.

Record Category. If the key is for a record category class, the procedure will return one of the field accessers. You have to say which field it is you want with the first argument:

```
: class_access(1, pair_key)([hello there]) =>
** hello
```

This is the same as the model procedure front, which accesses the first field of a pair. The access procedure will have an updater, so you can change the values inside the structures:

```
: vars x;
: [hello there] -> x;
: "goodbye" -> class_access(1, pair_key)(x);
: x =>
** [goodbye there]

: class_access(2, pair_key)([hello there]) =>
** [there]
```

This is the same as the procedure back, the other model for access procedures.

Non-record Category. Classes which don't have fields don't work with class_access: there's nothing to access, so there's no procedure it could return to do it. Neither do vector category classes: they have subscriptors intead. See class_subcr.

class_subscr(*KEY*) -> *PDR*;

Returns the subscripting procedure for a vector category class.

Vector Category. If the key is for a vector category class, it returns the subscripting procedure for that class. This is a procedure for getting at the elements of the structure:

```
: class_subscr(vector_key)(2, {hello there}) =>
** there
```

This is the same as the model procedure **subscrv** (which should have been called **subscrvector**). It takes two arguments: the first is the subscript of the element you want to change, and the second is the structure. The subscriptors always have updaters.

Non-vector Category. Classes which don't have fields don't work with **class_subscr**: there's nothing to subscript so there's no procedure it could return to do it. Neither do record category classes: they have access procedures intead. See **class_access**.

class_apply(*KEY*) -> *PDR*;

Returns the procedure which knows how to apply objects of the class. At base, the system only knows how to apply procedures, everything else is built from that.

You have seen that applying a vector is the same as using **subscrv**:

```
: vars x;
: {hello there vector} -> x;
: x(2) =>
** there
: subscrv(1, x) =>
** hello
```

The class apply for vectors, strings, words and pairs are set up to be the subscripting procedures **subscrv**, **subscrs**, **subscrw** and **subscrl**. Here's the vector case:

```
: class_apply(vector_key) =>
** <procedure subscrv>
```

But you can't apply a number. What happens is that the class apply procedure does exist, but it is a procedure which makes a mishap, perhaps called **sys_apply_error**:

```
: class_apply(integer_key) =>
** <procedure sys_apply_error>
```

It is possible to change the class applying procedures for the built-in types, and it is extremely useful for user-defined types. However, don't change the ones for vectors, strings, words or pairs.

When you write an expression like the **x(2)** above, what happens is that it gets dealt with in the normal way, which is this:

```
PUSHQ       2
CALL        "x"
```

But you can think of it as being:

```
PUSHQ       2
PUSHQ       "x"
CALL        "apply"
```

Assuming a procedure **reallyapply** which applied procedures directly, you can think of apply as being defined like this:

```
define apply(item);
    if isprocedure(item) then
        reallyapply(item);
    else
        class_apply(datakey(item))(item);
    endif
enddefine;
```

class_dataword(*KEY*) -> *WORD*;

Returns the name of the class. Every class has a name, which is a word. You can use this for whatever purpose you like: the system uses it for printing objects in the default format.

```
: class_dataword(procedure_key) =>
** procedure
: class_dataword(boolean_key) =>
** boolean
```

class_= (*KEY*) -> *PDR*;

Returns the class equality tester. The usual procedure **=** which has been used throughout this book just defers the work to one of the class equality testers.

You can think of **=** being defined like this:

```
define 7 =(left, right);
    class_=(datakey(right))(left, right)
enddefine;
```

(Note: the 7 is what makes it an infix operator. This is decribed in a later chapter.)

Don't try to change the equality testers for the built-in classes. But it's permissible to change them for any user-defined classes you may have.

The default value for the equality tester, for all classes, is a procedure called sys_=, which does a lot of work with the identity procedure == to decide if two objects are equal.

You can think of sys_= as being defined like this, but with the blanks filled in:

```
define sys_=(a, b);
    if a == b then
        return(true);
    endif;
    unless datakey(a) == datakey(b) then
        return(false);
    endunless;
    if datakey(a) == pair_key then
        sys_=(front(a), front(b)) and
        sys_=(back(a), back(b))
    elseif datakey(a) == vector_key then
        ...
    elseif ...
    elseif ...
    else
        false
    endif
enddefine;
```

CHAPTER 10

More Data Structures

The previous chapters covered general issues about data classes, and went into some depth about the most important data types in POP-11: words, booleans, numbers, lists and procedures, and how the data classes all tie together with keys. This chapter covers the remainder of the data types. On a first read, you might like to skip this chapter, in order to concentrate on the more important ones.

Vectors

Vectors are similar to lists, in that they are ordered sequences of arbitrary objects: the real difference is in their internal organisation, and hence the operations which can be performed on them. Syntactically, you form vectors exactly like lists, except you use braces (usually called curly brackets) instead of brackets (usually called square brackets). You should refer to the section on lists for more information; this section just highlights some of the features. Here is a vector of five objects:

```
: {one two three four five} =>
** {one two three four five}
```

As with lists, you may put any kind of object inside a vector. Here's a vector of lists of vectors:

```
: {{0} [0 0] [0 0 0]} =>
** {{0} [0 0] [0 0 0]}
```

Unlike the empty list, the empty vector has no special characteristics.

Just as with lists, words inside a vector do not represent variable references; instead, they are simply words. You can get the value of a variable by preceding its name with an up-arrow. And you can use the percent notation to have an evaluated section of the vector.

The most useful thing you can do with vectors is subscript them numerically, as you can with lists: this is the most natural operation to perform on vectors. Don't forget that the subscript of the first element of lists and vectors is 1, not zero. Subscripting is most useful if you remember that you can update the elements too. The following example shows a way of associating words with numbers:

```
: vars vec;
: {one two three} -> vec;
: vec(2) =>
** two
: "deux" -> vec(2);
: vec(2) =>
** deux
```

While a list is a chain of objects, a vector is a fixed number of objects. Figure 10.1 should make this clearer: the structure at the top is a list, the one at the bottom is a vector, and the ones in the middle are words. Notice that the elements of the list are identical to the elements of the vector, as they are words. But, of course, the vector is quite distinct from the list.

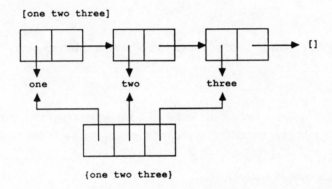

Fig. 10.1

From Figure 10.1 you should see that the list is made up from pairs, which are structures which contain exactly two elements. A vector is a structure which contains exactly some number of elements, which can be zero, one, or as many as wanted. But the number of elements in a particular vector is fixed when it is made.

Vector Procedures

Apart from making vectors with the curly bracket notation, you can also make them procedurally.

initv(*NUM*) -> *VEC*;

Builds a vector of the length given by the argument, and returns it. The resulting vector will have the word **undef** in all its positions. The requested length must be a valid length for a vector: an integer which is not less than zero.

consvector(*NUM*) -> *VEC*;

> Builds a vector of the given length the same as initv, and then takes *NUM* objects off the stack and puts them into the vector. The top of stack (last object pushed) will be the rightmost element of the vector; that is, the one with the highest subscript. The requested length must be an integer not less than zero.

And instead of getting access to the elements with the subscripting notation, you can do it with a procedure.

VEC(*NUM*) -> *RES*;

> Returns the *NUM*th element of the vector. This will mishap if the number is not a valid subscript for the vector, that is, not an integer, zero, negative, or bigger than the length for the vector.

ITEM -> *VEC*(*NUM*);

> Changes the *NUM*th element of the vector to be *ITEM*. Mishaps if the subscript is invalid.

subscrv(*NUM*, *VEC*) -> *RES*;

> Returns the *NUM*th element of the vector *VEC*. This will mishap if the number is not a valid subscript for the vector (non-integer, zero, negative, or bigger than length of vector) or if the argument *VEC* is not a vector.

ITEM -> subscrv(*NUM*, *VEC*);

> Changes the *NUM*th element of the vector *VEC* to be *ITEM*. This will mishap if the number is not a valid subscript for the vector (non-integer, zero, negative, or bigger than length of vector) or if the argument *VEC* is not a vector.

Of course, vectors have a recogniser:

isvector(*ITEM*) -> *BOOL*;

> Returns a boolean indicating if the argument is a vector.

References

References are the simplest of all the structures, but are one of the more difficult to come to grasp the utility of. They are single-element records: that is, they are a type of structure which always holds just a single element, known as the *content*.

consref(*ITEM*) -> *REF*;

> Constructs a new reference, with *ITEM* as its content.

cont(*REF*) -> *CONTENT*;

Returns the content of a reference. Mishaps if *REF* isn't a reference.

CONTENT -> cont(*REF*);

Changes the content of the given ref to be *CONTENT*. Mishaps if *REF* isn't a reference.

You make a ref like this:

```
: vars r;
: consref("hello") -> r;
: r =>
** <ref hello>
```

As you see, refs print in default format, with their content.

You can get at this, or change it, like this:

```
: 123 -> cont(r);
: r =>
** <ref 123>
: cont(r) =>
** 123
```

It is worth learning the few procedures for manipulating references; they are simple enough to remember for when you need them.

One prominent use they have is where you want to share values between two places: the kind of thing which can produce the nasty bugs in the health warning previously referred to.

If you want to try shared structures, references are a good structure to start with, as they are so simple. Here's an example to try:

```
: vars a b r;
: consref("shared") -> r;
: [^r alpha] -> a;
: [^r beta] -> b;

: a =>
** [<ref shared> alpha]
: b =>
** [<ref shared> beta]

: "stillshared" -> cont(r);

: a =>
**[<ref stillshared> alpha]
: b =>
** [<ref stillshared> beta]
```

Of course, you get this behaviour with all structures in POP-11. If it confuses you, try drawing the box diagrams for what's going on. In this example, we could have done the same thing with a single-element list; but if there is only one shared object needed, references suggest themselves naturally.

This kind of programming can be very difficult to debug. It only works if the reference in the one place is identical to the reference in the other place. If, for some reason, you make your data objects incorrectly, then the symptoms will be obscure, as different parts of your program will implicitly assume that they are getting the same data as the other parts, when in fact they won't.

Recogniser:

isref(*ITEM*) -> *BOOL*;

Returns a boolean indicating if the argument is a reference or not.

Strings

An increasingly common use for computers is text manipulation, and, in common with most languages, POP-11 has a data type especially for collecting characters together in sequences, called *strings*.

Strings are just like vectors, except that the only objects which you can put in them are characters, as represented by numbers. You are referred to the notes about character codes in the section on words above.

Strings have their own syntax, based on the 'single quote', usually called a 'string quote'. You just quote the characters you want, and you've built a string:

```
: 'this is a string' =>
** this is a string
```

There are no rules about what characters you can have in a string: notice the spaces in the example. But there is obviously a difficulty with single quotes and newlines, so there is an 'escaping' mechanism, based on the backslash. This lets you put any character you like in a string:

```
\'    single quote
\\    backslash
\t    tab character
\n    newline
\r    carriage return
\(3) character with code 3
```

(For details of tabs, newlines, etc., see section on characters in Chapter 8). In the last form, you can put any valid character number inside the parentheses.

Here's an example of a string with a single quote in it: a very common usage because single quotes are used for apostrophes:

```
: 'jonathan\'s backslash\\' =>
** jonathan's backslash\
```

Notice that strings print according to the characters that are in them, not according to how you have to type them in: 'a \ \b has length 3.

String Procedures

As with everything else, you can make strings procedurally. You can also subscript them with brackets, and the subscriptor has an updater.

inits(*NUM*) -> *STR*;

Builds a string of the given length, and returns it. The argument *NUM* must be an integral number, at least zero. Initally all the characters in the string will be the character whose code is zero.

consstring(*NUM*) -> *STR*;

Builds a string of the given length the same as **inits**, and then takes *NUM* character codes off the stack and puts them into the string. The top of stack (last object pushed) will be the rightmost element of the string; that is, the one with the highest subscript. The requested length must be an integer not less than zero.

STR(*NUM*) -> *CHAR*;

Returns the *NUM*th character from the string. Will mishap if the subscript is invalid: non-integral, less than one, or more than the length of the string.

CHAR -> *STR*(*NUM*);

Changes the *NUM*th character of the string to be *CHAR*. Will mishap if the subscript is invalid or the *CHAR* isn't a valid character code.

subscrs(*NUM*, *STR*) -> *CHAR*;

Returns the *NUM*th character from the string *STR*. Will mishap if the subscript is invalid (non-integral, less than one, or more than length of string) or if the argument *STR* isn't a string.

CHAR -> **subscrs**(*NUM*, *STR*);

Changes the *NUM*th character of the string *STR* to be the given *CHAR*. Will mishap if the subscript is invalid (non-integral, less than one, or more than length of string), if the argument *STR* isn't a string, or if *CHAR* isn't a valid character code.

One of the prime uses for strings is in manipulating the way objects are printed. This is because strings print exactly according to their characters. There is a most useful operator for turning objects into strings which are like their printed representation:

ITEM1 >< *ITEM2* -> *STR*;

Takes two arbitrary objects, and makes a string which consists of the characters which would have been printed for the two of them. This procedure is known as 'string concatenate'.

This last procedure might need an example: here we take the empty list and a number, and join them into a string. Notice the length of the string:

```
: vars s;
: [] >< 123 -> s;
: length(s) =>
** 5
: s =>
** []123
: datalist(s) =>
** [91 93 49 50 51]
```

isstring(*ITEM*) -> *BOOL*;

Returns a boolean indicating if the argument was a string or not.

Arrays

The array is a classic data type which is used for storing objects and accessing them by numbers. In this, they are very similar to vectors; the main differences are that arrays can use more than one number to find the object, and the internal structure is different.

For a typical use, consider representing a television picture. We can represent the screen as a rectangle of dots, each of a particular brightness – black and white only, for the moment.

To find the brightness of a particular dot, we would like to be able to do:

```
: tv(123, 5) =>
** 7
```

And this is what arrays are for. The *dimension* of an array is the number of numbers you need to access each location: the one above is two-dimensional. You can make arrays of any integral dimension which is one or more. A proper television program might use a four-dimensional array: across, down, colour, time.

In POP-11, each array has a list of bounds, which is the allowed range in each dimension. Our four-dimensional array might have bounds of 1 to 400 and 1 to 625 for the first two dimensions, 0 to 2 for the colour, and 1 to 24 for the time; this could fully store one second of British standard television.

You make arrays by giving a bounds list to the procedure **newarray**:

```
: vars fulltv;
: newarray([1 400 1 625 0 2 1 24]) -> fulltv;
: fulltv =>
** <array [1 400 1 625 0 2 1 24]>
```

You see that arrays print with angle brackets, and show their bounds list. When you first make an array, all the cells hold the word **undef**, as do vectors. Then you can access each element with the normal subscripting:

```
: fulltv(1, 1, 0, 1) =>
** undef
: 0 -> fulltv(1, 1, 0, 1);
```

Of course, initialising the array is tedious: so you can give an optional second argument to **newarray**, which instructs it to fill the array in a certain way.

newarray(*BOUNDS*) -> *ARR*;
newarray(*BOUNDS*, *INIT*) -> *ARR*;

Constructs a new array by the given bounds list *BOUNDS*. In the second form, *INIT* specifies the initial values of the cells. If it is a procedure, that procedure is run once for all the possible combinations of subscripts, and each result is put into the corresponding cell. If *INIT* isn't a procedure, it is used as the value for each cell. *INIT* may not be a list other than the empty list. If the first form is used (omitting *INIT*) then each cell will contain the word **undef. newarray** mishaps if the bounds list is misformed: it must be a list of integral numbers of even length, and in each pair of numbers, the first mustn't be bigger than the second.

The proper form for the bounds list is that it consists of pairs of numbers which are the lower bound and the upper bound for the dimensions of the array. Hence a two-dimensional array has a four-element bounds list. You can find out the bounds list of an array:

boundslist(*ARR*) -> *BOUNDS*;

Returns the bounds list of the given array, as was used when the array was constructed. Mishaps if *ARR* is not an array.

If you use the form where you give an initialiser which is a procedure, that procedure will be called for each cell of the array, with the appropriate arguments. Consider this example:

```
: vars ident3;

: define leaddiag(x, y);
:    if x = y then
:        1;
:    else
:        0;
:    endif;
: enddefine;

: newarray([1 3 1 3], leaddiag) -> ident3;
```

This would call **leaddiag** nine times, behaving as though you had done this:

```
: leaddiag(1, 1) -> ident3(1, 1);
: leaddiag(1, 2) -> ident3(1, 2);
: leaddiag(1, 3) -> ident3(1, 3);
: leaddiag(2, 1) -> ident3(2, 1);
: leaddiag(2, 2) -> ident3(2, 2);
: leaddiag(2, 3) -> ident3(2, 3);
: leaddiag(3, 1) -> ident3(3, 1);
: leaddiag(3, 2) -> ident3(3, 2);
: leaddiag(3, 3) -> ident3(3, 3);
```

Any procedure which you give as an initialiser should take as many arguments as there are dimensions of the array.

Notes on Arrays

Arrays can be big. Arrays take up as much space as needed for all the elements. This means that for an array like **fulltv** the storage requirements can be huge: that one takes 18 million cells, and probably won't fit on your computer. Similarily, they can take an incredible amount of processing time. If you want a big array where most of the cells contain the same thing, you want a thing called a 'sparse array', which only stores the unusual elements. Your system may have a library package for these, or you could write one. Another way of paring down the storage needed for arrays is to restrict the values the cells can have, perhaps to small numbers: consult your system documentation to see if this is possible on your system.

Arrays are subscripted by numbers. Sometimes, you might want to use other subscripts than numbers. For example, you might want a two-dimensional array where the subscripts are people's names and names of family relationships. POP-11 arrays are no good for this: you will have to write your own mechanism, possibly using properties (see below): however, these stuctures are often sparse, and a sparse array package might help, or an enumerated-type subscripting package. Consult your documentation.

Arrays are stored in a particular way. POP-11 arrays are implemented by using a piece of memory which is large enough to hold all the objects. The cells are arranged so that if you ran along the memory and wrote down the subscripts of each cell, the rightmost subscripts would change fastest. For example, consider an array whose bounds list is [0 9 0 19 0 11]; used for converting old British money to new. The order of the cells is exactly in ascending value: first £0 0s 0d, then £0 0s 1d up to £0 0s 11d, then £0 1s 0d and so on up to £9 19s 11d. This is called 'lexicographic' or 'row-major' order. The point of this is that it will probably be fastest if you access the memory in sequence (up or down) rather than pick items out at random. The effect is only really noticeable on large arrays on computers with some form of paging system or virtual memory: most minicomputers. Your POP-11 system may have methods for changing the storage order; look for the system variable poparray_by_row.

Arrays have been extensively researched. Because arrays are a classical data structure, and used in many computationally expensive programs (such as matrix arithmetic, computer vision, cartography), they have been examined in much detail. This means that many ways of implementing different forms of them have been found, and your system may provide a great deal of flexibility in their generation and use. Particular areas of interest include storage requirements, access speed, arrays where large areas are known to contain the same thing, where large areas won't be accessed very often, or where only a few different values are needed for each location. You should consult your system documentation for details: try looking up newanyarray and bitmaps for starters.

Arrays may not be primitive. Some versions of POP-11 implement arrays out of procedures and vectors, as this is a simple way of getting the facilities. The only problems this could possibly cause are that arrays are considered to be procedures by isprocedure, and that you could be misled about their size by datasize.

Properties

Many a program needs to associate one object with another. One classical solution is to have lists of even length which go [thing associate thing associate ...] and find the associate of a given thing using matches. The problem with this is that the time taken to find the associate is dependent on the number of things in your table. A classical method for reducing the amount of time to achieve this task is called 'hashing', and this is what POP-11's properties do.

The characteristics of a property are

1. It is the association between 'things' and their associates.

2. There is a default associate, which is the associate of all things not otherwise mentioned.

3. The number of things which are 'otherwise mentioned' can change as much as you like; the associate of any thing can be changed as your program runs.

4. The time taken to find the associate of a thing can be arranged so that it doesn't depend on how many things are 'otherwise mentioned'.

5. Finding the thing of an associate can be very, very slow.

6. Recognition is done with identity, not equality.

A typical use of POP-11 properties is to associate words to the number of times they appear in a document, which might be used like this:

```
: count("dog") =>
** 5
: count("prevaricates") =>
** 0
: count("aardvark") + 1 -> count("aardvark");
```

This would be arranged so that every item would have a count ('associate') of zero, unless it needed to be otherwise. You make properties with the procedure newproperty, which takes four, rather intricate, arguments:

```
: vars count;
: newproperty([], 100, 0, true) -> count;
: count =>
** <property>
```

Before explaining the meanings of the arguments in detail, this is what the arguments mean in this example. The **[]** means that there are no initial associations. The 100 means that we want 100 cells in this property; a good default value. The 0 is the value for all objects for which we haven't stored a different value. The true indicates that this is a permanent property; use this until you're sure you understand when not to.

Initial associations. You can give a list of initial associations. For example, to say that you want 5 to be the associate of dog, and 2 to be the associate of cat, you could do:

```
: newproperty([dog 5 cat 2], ...) -> count;
```

and this would have the same effect as doing

```
: newproperty([], ...) -> count;
: 5 -> count("dog");
: 2 -> count("cat");
```

Table size. Clearly, the property must have a table of all the 'otherwise mentioned' objects. This number controls the size of the that table. But it is *not* a limit on how many things you can put in that table. Instead, it just changes how fast you can find things. The way properties work is that you have a number of buckets to put things in. When you need to add something to the table, you add it (with its associate) to one of the buckets: you decide which one by running a 'hashing function' on it. When you need to look something up, you run the hashing function on it, and thus select one of the buckets, and run through all the objects in that bucket to see if it is in the table. If it is, look at the stored associate; if it isn't, return the default associate. Very roughly speaking, you should have about twice as many buckets as the number of objects you think you'll need in the table. If you make the number too small, it just works slower; too big, it wastes space. Don't worry too much about the size, though.

Default value. This is the associate for all objects which aren't stored in the table. In the counting example, the sensible value was zero, as this is the number of occurrences of words we haven't met in our document yet. In a property of names and phone numbers, you might like to use <false> to indicate people for whom you don't have a phone number.

Permanence flag. There are two kinds of properties, temporary and permanent. In a permanent property, the references to the 'things' (as opposed to the associates) will stay there forever. In a temporary property, 'things' which are not referenced elsewhere which count as garbage, and so get garbage collected, along with the reference to their associates. If this sounds beyond you, then you want a permanent property.

As mentioned in other places, POP-11 is a system which looks after the storage requirements for you: it builds structures as you need them. The flip side of this is that it reclaims space from objects you don't need any more: a process called 'garbage collection'. In essence, the only things you need are variables, the objects on the stack, values of variables, and anything referenced by these, even indirectly. Because you could never refer to anything else, their storage is up for grabs: they are garbage.

Sometimes properties are used to store information about objects which are only needed for a short time, and you want the entry in the property to be garbage collected along with the object. Such a property is called 'temporary'. The other kind is permanent. An example of a temporary property would be where a procedure stores in a property all the arguments it has ever had, with their results, so that it doesn't have to do the work again if it is called with the same argument. (Called a 'memofn' or memory procedure.) In this case, if there was no other reference to an object except as a thing in the property, you would never need to look it up again; so the property could be temporary.

On the other hand, if it was storing the arguments in the property so that you could later look at them, the property must be permanent, or else things could disappear without your knowing. On the other hand, if you make a property permanent when it could have been temporary it merely goes slower and uses more memory. In general, therefore, you should err on the side of safety, and regard temporary properties as dangerous, and always use permanent ones unless you *know* it should be temporary.

The reason why properties are fast is because of the hashing algorithm, which is based on the machine representation of the object. This means that structures (complex objects) are treated as the address of the piece of memory which they occupy: hence, all comparisons are done with identity. This limits the things which you can easily put in a property, for normal purposes. For example, you couldn't build a phrasebook structure very easily: the natural thing to do would be:

```
: [deux cent] -> french([two hundred]);
```

But this wouldn't have the desired effect, because lists, in general, aren't identical:

```
: [two hundred] == [two hundred] =>
** <false>
```

The reason for this, to repeat, is that the lists are made whenever needed. In this example, two lists were needed, and so two were made, and so they aren't identical.

The solution? Use structures which are inherently unique (booleans, integers, the empty list), which are kept unique by the system (words), or which you have kept a hold of (values of variables, elements of structures). If there is no way to do that, you won't be able to use properties in this way. To do the phrasebook example, you might try something like

```
: "deux_cent" -> french("two_hundred");
```

Property Procedures

It is possible to find the objects stored in the table of a property:

appproperty(*PROP, PDR*);

Calls the given procedure *PDR* on each object and its associate of the property *PROP*. *PDR* will be called like this:

PDR(*OBJECT, ASSOCIATE*);

Any results which the procedure returns will be left on the stack when **appproperty** finishes.

isproperty(*ITEM*) -> *BOOL*;

Returns a boolean indicating whether the argument was a property or not.

A note: properties are implemented in some systems as procedures. This means that **isprocedure** returns <true> when given a property.

Termin

For those final moments, a terminating object. This is used as an 'ending' object: perhaps the only common use is for procedures which read and write to files.

Character producing procedures (described elsewhere) are those which return a character code (number) each time they are called, corresponding to subsequent characters in a file on disk. When there are no more characters in the file, the character producer will return <termin>. Like the booleans, <termin> cannot be referenced directly: instead, there is a constant called **termin**, whose value is the <termin> object.

Imagine the variable **charprod** has been assigned a procedure which is a character producer for a very short file:

```
: charprod() =>
** 99
: charprod() =>
** 97
: charprod() =>
** 116
: charprod() =>
** <termin>
```

You might often see a construction like this:

```
until (charprod() ->> c) = termin do
    ...
enduntil;
```

This is the most common way of reading all the characters in a file. Notice the use of the constant **termin** and the double-headed assignment arrow.

Undefs

One of the most common programming errors is forgetting to initialise variables. In order to help with this, POP-11 always sets variables to a unique value when they are declared: the value is an 'undef' object. These are only made for newly declared variables, and there is no other way to get them. An undef object has a single element, which is the name of the variable it was made for: this helps track down the miscreant.

Example:

```
: vars silly list;
: silly =>
** <undef silly>
: [^silly] -> list;
: list =>
** [<undef silly>]
```

This shows that when **silly** was first declared, its value was the undef object <**undef silly**>. Then **silly** was used. At some point later, we see that there is this undef object in a list: almost certainly there is a bug somewhere in your program. Equally, the problem is that you took the value of **silly** before you initialised it to something sensible.

isundef(*ITEM***) -> ***BOOL***;**

Returns a boolean indicating if the argument was an undef object or not.

User-Defined Types

Even with so many built-in data types, you may find it convenient to define your own. Usually the advantages are that the type will have names appropriate to your application, and you can test for them explicitly. You will find that all the general procedures such as **length** will work on your new types.

There are two basic methods for defining new types. The first is more primitive and not so often used. It uses a procedure called **conskey**: refer to your system documentation if you are interested. The second method is much simpler, has nice syntax, and provides most of the facilities you might need.

Refer to the previous chapter for the classification of structures into vector and record category classes.

Vector Category Classes

To make a new class of variable size objects, just decide the name of the object. Suppose you want a type called 'box':

   : **vectorclass box;**

This makes everything you need. You get five procedures: a recogniser, a constructor, a subscriptor, and two procedures for making and accessing the contents in a convenient way. In this example, they will be called **isbox**, **initbox**, **subscrbox**, **consbox**, and **destbox**. The names of procedures are always formed from the name of the type (**box**) and the prefixes as in the examples. The procedures work like the ones for vectors: see section above.

isbox(*ITEM***) -> ***BOOL***;**

Returns a boolean indicating if the item is of type box or not.

initbox(*NUM*) -> *BOX*;

Returns a box of the given size. This will cause a mishap if the size is negative or not an integer. See also **consbox** below.

subscrbox(*NUM*, *BOX*) -> *ITEM*;

Returns one of the elements of the given box, which are numbered from 1 to the size of the box. This will mishap if the argument *BOX* isn't of type box, or if the number is less than 1, not an integer, or bigger than the given box. This procedure has an updater:

ITEM -> subscrbox(*NUM*, *BOX*);

Changes the specified element of the given box to be the given item. Mishaps as above.

consbox(*NUM*) -> *BOX*;

This is for making a box from items already on the stack. The argument is the size of the box you want to make, and it assumes that you have already placed that many objects on the stack to fill it with. The first object you put on the stack will have the lowest subscript.

Here's an example of making a box of three items:

```
: vars box;
: "a", "b", "c", consbox(3) -> box;
: subscrbox(1, box) =>
** a
```

This procedure could have been defined like this:

```
define consbox(n) -> box;
vars box i;
    initbox(n) -> box;
    for i from 1 to n do
        -> subscrbox(i, box);
    endfor;
enddefine;
```

destbox(*BOX*) -> *ITEMS*;

This is for putting all the items in a box onto the stack, followed by the length of the box. Using the box from the previous example:

```
: destbox(box) =>
** a b c 3
```

This procedure could have been defined like this:

```
define destbox(box);
vars i;
    for i from 1 to length(box) do
        subscrbox(i, box);
    endfor;
    length(box);
enddefine;
```

Vector class objects behave much the same as vectors. So, by default, the class apply procedure will be the subscriptor: so these two calls have the same effect:

```
subscrbox(2, box) =>
box(2) =>
```

Vector class objects print in POP-11's 'default style', like this:

```
: box =>
** <box a b c>
```

You may find this unsuited to your application. You should be able to change this, and other aspects of your new types as described in the preceding chapter.

Of course, your new types will have a key and a dataword: the dataword will be the word **box** and the key will be unique.

Record Category Classes

Where you need a data type which has a fixed number of elements, you need a record class object. Common examples of this are phone numbers (area code and number), people in family trees (name, mother, father), or geographic features of towns (name, latitude, longitude).

Making these is very nearly as easy as with **vectorclass**; but here you have to decide on the names of the procedures for accessing the elements of the record. For an example, we use towns:

```
: recordclass town name latitude longitude;
```

This makes three general procedures, and one for each field of the record. The general procedures are a recogniser, a constructor, and a destructor; in this case called **istown**, **constown** and **desttown**. The access procedures are called **name**, **latitude** and **longitude**. The general procedures are always formed from the prefixes **is**, **cons** and **dest**, while the access procedures always have the names you gave in the **recordclass** statement.

To give you a model for these procedures, consider pairs. These are two-element records whose accessing procedures are called **front** and **back**; so it could have been defined like this:

```
: recordclass pair front back;
```

Here's how the 'town' procedures work:

istown(*ITEM*) -> *BOOL*;

Returns a boolean indicating if the argument is of type 'town' or not.

constown(*NAME, LAT, LONG*) -> *TOWN*;

Returns a town made from the arguments. Constructor procedures will always have the same number of arguments as there are fields in your record. Our 'town' records have three fields, so **constown** takes three arguments.

desttown(*TOWN*) -> *LONG* -> *LAT* -> *NAME*;

Returns all the elements of a town. Destructor procedures always return the same number of results as there are fields in the record. This will mishap if the argument isn't of the right type.

name(*TOWN*) -> *NAME*;
latitude(*TOWN*) -> *LAT*;
longitude(*TOWN*) -> *LONG*;

These procedures access the different fields of the record. They mishap if they are not given a 'town' type object. They all have updaters, and so can be used like this:

ITEM -> **name**(*TOWN*);
ITEM -> **latitude**(*TOWN*);
ITEM -> **longitude**(*TOWN*);

When you give the **recordclass** statement, you give the names and number of these procedures.

Record class objects print in default format – see the notes under Vector Class above for suggestions on this.

Special Fields

Both vector and record class objects can be defined with variations. These are to do with the kinds of objects which will go into their fields, and the status of the procedures they make.

Normally, all structures in POP-11 can have any object as an element; this is a key feature of the language. Occasionally, it is useful to be able to restrict the types of object which can be stored in a structure. The major use is to save space.

Both **vectorclass** and **recordclass** take optional 'field specifications', for restricting the fields to hold only certain sizes of integers. A field specification can be:

The word full:

> This is the normal (default) specification, and means that the field is a 'full field' and can hold any POP-11 object whatsoever.

A positive integer:

> This restricts the size of the field to be a number of bits; the field can only hold numbers which will fit into this number of bits. If you give an integer n, the field will only be able to hold the integers from 0 to 2^n-1. For example, if you specify 3, the field will be able to take the integers 0 to 7.

A negative integer:

> Similar to giving a positive integer, but the fields can hold negative integers too. If you specify the integer $-n$, then the fields can hold the integers -2^{n-1} to $2^{n-1}-1$. For example, if you give -3, the field will be able to take the integers -4 to 3.

The word decimal:

> (If your system supports floating point numbers.) This restricts the value of the field to be a single-precision floating point value. See section on Numbers for more information.

The word ddecimal:

> (If your system supports floating point numbers.) This restricts the value of the field to be a double-precision floating point number. See section on Numbers for more information.

Field Specifications in Use

With recordclass, you can add a field specification after each of the field names by preceding it by a colon, like this:

```
: recordclass chesspiece ident colour:1 rank:3 file:3;
```

This would make a type which you could use to represent the pieces on a chessboard. The first field, the identifier, might be words such as blackbishop, or pawn4. The second field could be either 0 or 1 for black and white. The rank and file of the piece gives its coordinates; we can make these small fields because we know we can represent the whole board with these numbers.

With vectorclass, you can add a field specification after the name, like this:

```
vectorclass bitvector 1;
```

This would make a type which you could use to represent black and white graphics images.

Some points about field specifications: in general, their use tends to be unhelpful. It is one of the great strengths of POP-11 that you can put arbitrary types in any field of any structure: by restricting fields in this way, you lose that power. For example, in the chess piece as shown above, what happens when a piece is taken? Without the field specification, you could simple put <false> in the coordinates. With the restrictions, it becomes uglier. (One possibility is to add a field of a single bit to say if it is on the board.) Their main use is to save space in memory, and so they are sometimes invaluable. For example, to hold a 1000 by 1000 two-level graphics image in vectors (in the simplest method) would take some 4 megabytes in most computers POP-11 runs on. If each pixel only takes one bit, then this is reduced to 128 kilobyte. This may make the difference between the program being able to run or not on your machine.

CHAPTER 11

Syntax, IO, and Compilation

Introduction

Throughout this book the syntax of POP-11 has been presented in a slightly simplified form. This is because the rules have been designed to give a language which reads easily: unfortunately, this makes the rules look a little complicated.

In fact, the syntax rules of POP-11 are quite straightforward, and have a simple unified framework. This chapter presents the syntax and related issues.

Streams

In common with many languages and operating systems, POP-11 uses the idea of input and output streams. These are essentially places for getting and putting characters. In normal use, the input stream will be your keyboard, and the output stream will be your screen.

When you compile a file, the main thing that happens is that POP-11 changes its input stream to be the file, temporarily. After the whole file has been read, the input stream returns to what it was before – usually your keyboard.

Itemisation

Whenever the POP-11 system is reading your program, or any other input, it breaks it up into chunks called 'items'. There are three basic kinds of items: words, strings, and numbers.

There is a procedure **itemread** (of no arguments) which reads the next item from the input stream. The statement above, that there are three kinds of item, means that **itemread** normally returns either a word, a string, or a number. When the input stream is exhausted, **itemread** returns the special object <termin>.

Pretend that we have arranged (somehow) for **itemread** to be reading from a file which looks like this:

```
define silly();
    'hello', 3, "foo";
enddefine;
```

How many items are there? Successive calls of **itemread** would return these values:

1.	define	word
2.	silly	word
3.	(	word
4.	)	word
5.	;	word
6.	hello	string
7.	,	word
8.	3	number
9.	,	word
10.	"	word
11.	foo	word
12.	"	word
13.	;	word
14.	enddefine	word
15.	;	word
16.	<termin>	special object

Note that this is quite different from loading the file – all we are doing here is reading the items in it. There are a few special things to note about the itemisation. Firstly, 'white space' (a space, tab or new line) always marks the end of an item, but item boundaries also occur in other places.

The definitive rules on 'quoted word' syntax are given in the data types chapter. POP-11 always follows those rules when itemising. Strings are always surrounded by string quotes. Numbers always begin with either a minus sign, or a digit.

What you should be able to understand from this is where you must have spaces in your programs, and where they are allowed:

Must: Between words which would otherwise join into a single word according to the quoted word rules. For example,

define silly	two words
definesilly	one word

After an alphabetic word which precedes a number:

[now we are 6]	a list of three words then a number
[now we are6]	a list of three words

Where you want spaces in strings:

'once upon a time'

Must Not: In the middle of single words:

end define   two words

Where you don't want spaces in strings:

'cheapertelegramsaredonelikethis'

May: Anywhere else, between the items. This is perfectly understandable by POP-11, if not by people:

```
define fac                                      (
    x
);if x
=                                         0 then
1                       else fac(
x
-                                              1
)*x
endif enddefine;
```

Lists Are Not Items

It would seem sensible for lists to be items, but they are not. A file which contained just this:

```
define foo(x);
    [^x]
enddefine;
```

would have 12 items. The syntax for making the list [^x] comes back as the four items: the two brackets, the up-arrow and x.

Numbers

POP-11 has many kinds of numbers, as described in the data types chapter. The syntax for the basic set breaks down into five different kinds:

Integer format. The simplest: just some digits, possibly preceded by a minus sign.

1234   -4321

Floating Point format. Characterised by having a decimal point in the middle. There must be at least one digit on each side of the point.

0.0   -123.0   3.141592

Exponential format. Characterised by having a lowercase 'e' in the middle. There must be at least one digit on each side of the 'e', and the number on the left can be in floating point format.

```
1e3        6.023e-23        -0.00003e12
```

Non-Decimal formats. Many people use other number bases other than ten. In POP-11, you can specify numbers in other bases by putting the base in front of the number, followed by a colon, like this:

```
16:F1D0        same as 61904 in decimal
```

If this looks useless, skip this section. If it looks obvious, skip the explanation.

In ordinary, base-10 numbers, each digit is written in a column which has a value which is a power of 10, like this:

10^2 10^1 10^0 10^{-1} 10^{-2}
  1   2   3   .   4   5

The value of the number is found by multiplying each digit by the value for its column, and adding these together. The number above is

$$123.45 = (1 \times 10^2) + (2 \times 10^1) + (3 \times 10^0) +$$
$$(4 \times 10^{-1}) + (5 \times 10^{-2}) \; = 100 + 20 + 3 + 0.4 + 0.05$$

For this to make sense, you have to know that $10^{-x} = 1/10^x$, and $10^0 = 1$.

Well, you can write numbers in a different base, simply by substituting a different number for all the 10s above. Normally, you use whole positive numbers, and POP-11 restricts you to this. Normally, you only use digits which are less than the base; POP-11 restricts you to this too. If you need digits which are more than 9, you use upper case letters: A for 10, B for 11, and so on. So the example number is worked out like this:

16^3 16^2 16^1 16^0
  F   1   D   0

$$= (15 * 16^3) + (1 * 16^2) + (13 \times 16^1) + (0 \times 16^0)$$
$$= 61440 \quad + 256 \quad + 208 \quad + 0$$
$$= 61904$$

Some notes: the base is always given in decimal. You can use the 'fractional point' (née decimal point), and so 2:0.1 is equal to 0.5, and you can even use exponential notation, so 5:10e2 is equal to 125. The highest base you can use is 36, as the only characters POP-11 will recognise as digits are the ten 'proper' digits, and the 26 uppercase letters. One use of this is to code text up in a very compact way, or to make large numbers quickly. Try your name like this: 36:JONATHAN.

Character Numbers. The last format for numbers is very simple: backquotes around a character stand for the character code for that character. For example:

```
: `j` =>
** 106
```

In the places where you need it, this is invaluable. You can use all the 'quoting' mechanisms for strings in between the character quotes, for when you need the character number for unprintable characters. In particular, note these examples:

'\"   to get the backquote itself
'\ \'   to get the backslash

Words as Identifiers

To get a full understanding of POP-11, it is necessary to have an idea of the processes which go on behind the scenes in your system; how the compilation proceeds from your input.

You will have noticed that the only objects which ever represent another *within* POP-11 are words. As far as POP-11 is concerned, all the other data types are just representing themselves. Of course, to the programmer, they are representing objects in the world, or numbers, or whatever.

Words have two basic attributes: the characters which make up their name, and their 'identprops', or identifier properties. We can distinguish several different uses of words by their identprops: undefined words, ordinary 'name' words, operator words, macro words, and syntax words. There is a procedure called identprops for finding out which of these classes a particular word is in.

identprops(*WORD*) -> *IDENTSPEC*;
    For discovering the identifier properties of a word. Mishaps if the argument isn't a word. The *IDENTSPEC* is one of:
    (a) The integer 0 for ordinary 'name' words.
    (b) The word undef for words with no identifier.
    (c) Some other number for operator words. (See notes below)
    (d) The word macro for macro words.
    (e) The word syntax for syntax words. (See notes below)

Ordinary 'Name' Words

All of the words which have been declared to be a variable are 'names' for the variable. This includes all the names of your procedures, as well as your variables, as well as all the procedures and variables in the system. All name words have a value, which you use in the normal way. The 'ordinariness' is contrasted against the operator, macro and syntax words.

For example:

```
: vars foo;
: identprops("foo") =>
** 0
```

Words with no identifier

Some words have no other function than being a data object which prints in a convenient way, and is different from all others. This kind of word has never been declared in any way (**define**, or **vars**, or **constant**) and has always been used in word quotes, or inside lists. For example, if they weren't declared elsewhere, the words in this list would be words with no identifier:

```
: [hello there] =>
** [hello there]
: identprops("there") =>
** undef
```

Operators

Operators are very much like ordinary variable names, except that the syntax for their use is different. Remember how you use procedures such as **+** and **matches** by putting their name between their arguments, like this:

```
: 3 + 4 =>
** 7
```

Procedures such as these two are operators. For words which have been declared as operators, **identprops** returns their precedence, which is an indication of how tightly they group their arguments.

Consider the expression:

```
: 3 + 4 * 5 =>
```

Is this (3 + 4) * 5 which evaluates to 35, or is it 3 + (4 * 5), which evaluates to 23? In POP-11, the operators are evaluated in order of their precedences. If you try **identprops** on "*" and "+", you will find that they have precedences of 4 and 5 respectively. This means that * will always be evaluated before + in an expression like the example above: it is equal to 23. If you want the addition to be done first, you have to write

```
: (3 + 4) * 5 =>
** 35
```

People are not good at remembering the order of evaluation of different operators.

Experience shows that arithmetic expressions are fairly safe, all others need brackets. To reiterate the good advice given in other textbooks (and without which this one would be incomplete), if you ever find any confusion whatsoever, add the brackets. They won't slow your program down, and they'll ensure you get what you wanted.

Macros

Macros are a method for defining shorthand ways of writing bits of POP-11. Some people feel that they are a hindrance, and any properly written program will have no use for them. Others wouldn't be without them. When your program is being read, any macros are 'expanded' to their full form before anything else happens.

A typical use of this is during program debugging. You might have a macro called **DEBUG**, which is defined to print out some debugging information. When the program is finished, you change the definition for **DEBUG** so that it does nothing at all. In this way, your program text remains unchanged, but without the overhead of the debugging printing.

Syntax Words

All of POP-11's keywords are 'syntax words'. This is how POP-11 knows that it is to treat **define** differently from ordinary words such as your variable names.

All opening keywords, such as **define** and **if**, (but not **enddefine** or **then**) are syntax words whose value is a procedure. The basic plot of compiling POP-11 involves getting a keyword and doing the action for it. For example, the procedure which is the value of the keyword **if** is responsible for compiling all of the code up to and including the following **endif**. Of course, it will delegate much of the work to other procedures.

There is a special kind of syntax word which is the 'syntax operator'. This is used for some special keywords, such as parentheses, which interact with ordinary operators. The **identprops** of these is a word which begins with "syntax".

Compiling a Simple Procedure

In order to help you understand the compilation process, here is a worked example of compiling a simple procedure. You may like to refer to the chapter on virtual machine instructions before reading on.

The Basic Plot

The structure of the procedure which does most of the work is a bit like the following; the numbers at the right are just for reference as we work through the example.

```
define basicplot(closer);                                    0
vars item nextone;
    repeat forever
        itemread() -> item;                                  1
        if item = closer then                                2
            return();                                        3
        elseif identprops(item) = "syntax" then              4
            valof(item)();                                   5
        else
            nextitem() -> nextone;                           6
            if nextone = "(" then                            7
                we've found a procedure application           8
            else
                we're pushing a value                        9
            endif
        endif
    endrepeat
enddefine;                                                   10
```

As you see, we're forever reading items and seeing if they are syntax words. This outline doesn't show any of the error checking of the real version, anything to do with operators, or any of the complications to do with real life. But it suits the present purpose.

The Simple Procedure

Here's a procedure which returns a boolean indicating if its argument is the number 3 or not. Notice it has used = in the ordinary procedure position: this isn't usual, but it works, and makes the following explanation somewhat simpler.

```
define is3(thing) -> result;
    = (thing, 3) -> result;
enddefine;
```

Let's assume that this text is in a file, and we've arranged our input stream to be that file. As we've just started compiling, we want to compile a whole file, so we call basicplot with the special object <termin>, which is the last item we can read from the file. As we go along, little pieces of code will show the kind of thing the compiler will be checking, but with results printed out, so you can see what's happening.

The first thing we do is read an item, and we get **define**.

Then we check it against the closer, which is <**termin**>. It's not the same, so we go to line 4, and check its identprops. The identprops of **define** is **syntax**, so we do line 5, which is applying the value of the variable **define**.

Inside the procedure **define** we read the next item, which should be the name of the procedure we want to define. We get **is=3**, and declare it as a variable, just as though you had done

> **vars is3;**

Then **define** tries to find the arguments for this new procedure. We read another item, and get the opening bracket (. This tells **define** that we've come to the list of arguments. Get another item, this one is **thing**. As this is the name of our argument, we declare it and add it to our (so far empty) collection of arguments. Another item: a closing bracket). This tells **define** that we've come to the end of the argument list – we might have had a comma and then some more arguments. After the argument list comes the outputs, so we get another item: it's an assignment arrow, introducing the outputs. Another item, **result**, which we declare and add to our collection of output locals. Another item: a semicolon. This tells us that we've come to the end of the output locals.

At this point, we've collected one argument (**thing**) and one output (**result**). Now we can plant the first virtual instructions: one just to start the procedure off, and some to say that it has some local variables:

```
PROCEDURE
LOCAL      "thing"
LOCAL      "result"
```

As **thing** is an argument, we have to get that from the stack:

```
POP        "thing"
```

That's the 'prologue' of the procedure: just stuff to get the procedure going, deal with the arguments, and so on. Now for the body of the procedure.

The inside of a procedure definition is just like any other piece of POP-11 code: we just call **basicplot** again, but this time the closing item is the word **enddefine**.

So, there we are again at line 1: reading an item. We get the word **=**. This isn't our current closing word (**enddefine**), so we check its identprops, which isn't **syntax**, so we go to line 5.

Here we 'peek' at the next item to see if it is an opening bracket with the procedure **nextitem**. This looks at the next item coming, but still leaves it there so the next call of **itemread** will find it: a feature called lookahead. We found that the next item will be an opening bracket: this means we've found a procedure application. What we have to do is evaluate all the arguments (in this case, just push them) and then plant a call to **=**.

In essence, we can call **basicplot**, yet again. In case you're getting confused, we have a calling chain like this:

compilefile opened the file, and then called

    basicplot(termin) to compile to the end of it, which called

        define to compile the procedure, which compiled the header of the procedure, and then called

            basicplot("enddefine") to compile its body, which found a procedure call, and called

                basicplot(")") to compile the arguments

Which is as far as we got. **basicplot** reads the next item, which is the word **thing**, and gets to line 9 (not the closer, not syntax, not followed by an opening bracket) and plants the push for the item:

```
PUSH        "thing"
```

basicplot then gets the comma, which is a syntax word. The procedure for this doesn't do very much beyond getting past syntax checking. Then we get the **3**, which again we just push:

```
PUSHQ       3
```

Then we find the closing bracket, which is what the innermost call of **basicplot** was looking for. That call returns, and so we are inside the call of **basicplot** which is looking for **enddefine**.

When we left this call, we left to compile the arguments of a procedure application. That dealt with, we continue with line 8 and plant the call itself:

```
CALL        "="
```

Then we go back to the top of the loop to line 1, and read another item. We get the assignment arrow ->, which is a syntax word. The procedure for this reads an expression, which it compiles in updater mode. In its simplest case, like we have here, it just means we plant POPs instead of PUSHes. In its more complicated cases, it deals with expressions like

```
3 -> hd(list);
```

The assignment arrow reads the next item: the word **result**. It peeks at the next item, and because it isn't an opening parenthesis, decides we have the simple case and plants

```
POP         "result"
```

and returns. Back to **basicplot** looking for **enddefine** ...

We read the semicolon, which is another syntax word. Like the comma previously, it doesn't do much. Now we get **enddefine**, which causes this call of **basicplot** to finish, returning to the procedure **define**. Now, **define** knows that all its body has been compiled, so it just has to deal with its 'epilogue': the piece of code which tidies everything up and forms the end of the procedure we are building.

Because our new procedure **is3** has an output local, we must push the value of the output:

PUSH   "result"

And that's it: just a closing instruction to indicate the end:

ENDPROCEDURE

Somehow, we also get the new procedure into the variable **is3**, such as by actually *executing*, rather than just planting

POP   "is3"

Here are all the virtual instructions which got planted, next to numbers which indicate which bit of the source procedure caused them:

define is3(thing) -> result; =(thing, 3) -> result; enddefine;
1   2   3   4   5 6   7 8   9   10

1	PROCEDURE	
3	LOCAL	"thing"
4	LOCAL	"result"
3	POP	"thing"
6	PUSH	"thing"
7	PUSHQ	3
5	CALL	"="
8,9	POP	"result"
4	PUSH	"result"
10	ENDPROCEDURE	

1,2   -> is3;

As you have seen, while the actual detail of compiling even a simple procedure is involved, the basic principles are simple: read items, categorise them, execute syntax procedures, and plant virtual instructions.

Consumers and Producers

It should be clear that none of the discussion above required the original items to be coming from any particular place: any abstract 'stream' would do. And a stream was simply a place to get items from.

POP-11 has two basic classes of input and output: characters and items. And there are two basic kinds of procedures for dealing with these: repeaters and consumers.

A repeater is a procedure which has no arguments, and produces a single result. A consumer is a procedure which has a single argument, and produces no results.

So, the procedure itemread which was discussed above is an item repeater. A procedure such as pr, which prints a single item, is an item consumer.

However, it is clear that underneath itemread there must be a character repeater to produce the characters for it to turn into items. This underlying procedure is called cucharin, and is the procedure used to get characters whenever POP-11 wants to read its input, and is the one you should normally call to get characters.

Similarly, pr must have a procedure to consume the characters it wants to print. It does: cucharout. This is the procedure you should normally call if you want to output characters.

You can make your own consumers and producers, out of various objects. The most commonly used deal with disk files, although others deal with POP-11 structures. Before detailing the built-in procedures for manipulating this kind of procedure, here are details of what consumers and repeaters are like:

char_consumer(*CHAR*);

A character consumer is a procedure which takes a single argument, and returns no results. The argument must be a legitimate character code (integer). Each character is 'consumed' and goes to an appropriate place, which is dependent on the particular character consumer. Typically this will be a particular disk file, the user's screen, or something analogous. The only thing other than characters which the procedure will accept is the special object <termin>, which will perform a 'closing' action on the destination object. Typically this will be closing a disk file. Any other argument will cause the consumer to mishap.

char_repeater() -> *CHAR*;

A character repeater is a procedure which takes no arguments, and returns a single character code (integer) result. Each time it is called, it returns the next character from a place which is dependent on the particular character repeater. Typically this will be a disk file, the user's keyboard, or something analogous. The only other result the procedure might produce is the special object <termin>, which will be produced when the procedure can't get any more characters. Calling the procedure again after it has produced <termin> will generate a mishap.

item_consumer(*ITEM*);

An item consumer is a procedure which has a single argument, and produces no results. The argument can be any POP-11 object, and is sent to a place which depends on the particular procedure. If the argument is the special object <termin>, then the procedure will perform a closing action on the destination. Typically this will be closing a disk file or the user's screen. Any other object will be dealt with appropriately.

item_repeater( ) -> *ITEM*

An item repeater is a procedure which takes no arguments, and returns a single item. The item will always be one of these: a word, a string, a number, nil, or <termin>. Each time it is called, it will return the next item from a place which depends on the particular procedure. Typically this will be a disk file or the user's keyboard. When there are no more items available, the repeater will return <termin>. If it is called again after this, it will mishap.

There are a few special repeaters and consumers, which the system provides:

cucharin( ) -> *CHAR*;

Produces characters from the '*current character input*'. This is a variable whose value is normally **charin**, but can be changed as needed. See also the following section on simple IO techniques.

cucharout(*CHAR*);

Consumes characters, and sends them to the '*current character output*'. This is a variable which is normally set to **charout**. See the IO techniques section below for simple methods of using this.

charin( ) -> *CHAR*;

Produces characters from the 'standard input'. This is usually the user's keyboard, but is sometimes a file or other mechanism. For example, in the Unix operating system, you can invoke POP-11 like this:

```
% cat myfile | pop11
```

This would make the standard input come from the text in the file called **myfile**. Most operating systems have mechanisms like this.

charout(*CHAR*);

Consumes characters and sends them to the 'standard output'. This is usually the user's keyboard, but is sometimes a file or other mechanism. Most operating systems have a way of redirecting the output of programs, such as Unix's pipes:

```
% cat myfile | pop11 | sort > sorted
```

This would make POP-11 read its input from the text in the file **myfile**. All the output would go through the program **sort** (which sorts the lines of its input alphabetically) and all the sorted output would be put into a file called **sorted**.

rawcharin( ) -> *CHAR*;

This is a repeater which produces characters from the same place as **charin**, except in a 'raw' mode. This would only be different when reading from the user's keyboard: normally all input is echoed (so the users can see it as they type) and mistakes can be changed by pressing delete keys, and so on. In 'raw' mode, characters aren't echoed, and they are available as soon as they are typed. This is useful for writing screen editors, where the program must be able to, for example, take its own action for delete keys.

rawcharout(*CHAR* **);**

This is a consumer which sends its output to the same place as **charout**, except in a 'raw' mode. As for **rawcharin**, this is different in the amount of processing which happens to the characters. For example, many operating systems translate some characters into others when they are printed or put into files. In raw mode, less of this happens: of course this is highly system-dependent.

itemread( ) -> *ITEM*;

This produces items from the same place as **cucharin** produces characters. While reading these items, any macros are expanded. This calls **readitem** to get the items, then tests to see if they are macros.

readitem( ) -> *CHAR*;

This produces items from the same place as **cucharin** produces characters: it differs from **itemread** in that it doesn't expand macros. This calls **cucharin** to get the characters to form the items.

erase(*ANYTHING* **);**

While not strictly a consumer, it can be convenient to think of **erase** as an anything consumer. It takes a single argument, which disappears.

Imagine a procedure which takes two character consumer arguments, like this:

```
define bigjob(normal, errors);
   ...
enddefine;
```

Normally you'd pass this two proper character consumers, perhaps like this:

```
: bigjob(discout('good'), cucharout);
```

which would send all the normal output to the file **good**, and put all the error messages to your screen. You might want to ignore all the normal output, and keep the errors, like this:

```
: bigjob(erase, discout('bad'));
```

The only way **erase** behaves differently from a proper consumer is that it is not fussy about what it eats, and doesn't do anything special when given <termin> – it just eats that like everything else.

pr(*ANYTHING* **);**

This is the classic item consumer. It calls **cucharout** to get rid of the characters it wants to print.

discin(*FILENAME*) -> *CHARREP*;

The classic character repeater factory. The argument is a filename given as a string. The result is a character repeater procedure. **discin** will cause a mishap if it cannot open the file requested for any reason, such as misformed filename, non-existant file, insufficient access privileges.

discout(*FILENAME*) -> *CHARCONSU*;

The class character consumer factory. The argument is a filename given as a string. The result is a character consumer procedure. **discout** will mishap if it can't open the file requested for any reason, such as misformed filename, or insufficient access privileges. It *may* mishap if the file already exists: this depends on your operating system.

stringin(*STRING*) -> *CHARREP*;

The argument is any arbitrary string. The result is a character repeater which produces the characters from the string one at a time. It produces <termin> after the last character in the string.

incharitem(*CHARREP*) -> *ITEMREP*;

This is how to make item repeaters from character repeaters. The argument should be a procedure which is a character repeater. The result will be an item repeater. If *CHARREP* isn't a suitable procedure then *ITEMREP* will mishap when it is called.

outcharitem(*CHARCONSU*) -> *ITEMCONSU*;

This is how to make item consumers from character consumers. The argument should be a procedure which is a character consumer, and the result will be an item consumer along the lines of **pr**. If *CHARCONSU* isn't a suitable procedure, then *ITEMCONSU* will mishap when it is called.

Using POP-11's IO Procedures

From the descriptions above, it might not be readily apparent how to read and write files in POP-11. Here follow some simple procedures for doing just that.

First problem: just getting the printing into a file. Of course, you should just be able to use the editing environment of your system for simple tasks. But when you want your procedures to print to a file, it is straightforward.

Here's a procedure which takes an object, and prints it into a file:

```
define prtofile(item, filename);
vars cucharout;
    discout(filename) -> cucharout;
    item =>
    cucharout(termin);
enddefine;
```

To run it, you have to know that **discout** expects its filename to be as a string:

:   prtofile([hello there file], 'myfile');

You won't see anything, but if you're next to the right disk drive you might hear something. You'll have a file called **myfile**, and it will look like this:

** [hello there file]

As described above, **pr** always calls **cucharout** to deal with the individual characters, and the printarrow always calls **pr**. The key part here is making **cucharout** a local. Because of POP-11's dynamic scoping, any procedures called by **prtofile**, or called by anything it calls (and so on) will inherit the value given to it inside **prtofile**. Unless, of course, one of the called procedures changes it. And because the value is local, when **prtofile** returns, it will restore the previous value.

The **cucharout(termin)**; at the end closes the file. It isn't strictly necessary to do this, as the file will get closed eventually, but you can get into some confusing situations if you don't close it.

You want to have output going to your screen (or another file) at the same time. If so, what you want is something a bit more like the conventional file handling of other languages. Here are three procedures for opening, writing, and closing files. Normally, you wouldn't have a global **mycucharout**. Instead, it would be local to some high-level procedure responsible for printing.

```
vars mycucharout;

define openmyfile(filename);
    discout(filename) -> mycucharout;
enddefine;

define prtomyfile(item);
vars cucharout;
    mycucharout -> cucharout;
    pr(item);
enddefine;

define closemyfile();
    mycucharout(termin);
enddefine;
```

Second problem: reading from files. The simplest case is where you have perhaps a list structure which you want to save, and then get back another day. A very simple (but crude) method involves making a file with a simple POP-11 program in it, then compiling that file:

```
define writething(thing, filename);
vars cucharout;
    discout(filename) -> cucharout;
    pr(thing);
    pr(";");
    cucharout(termin);
enddefine;
```

This is just like the previous procedure, except it uses **pr** directly, rather than using the printarrow. This means it won't have the ** at the front. Now if your structure was just a list containing words, numbers or other lists, then it will print out in exactly the same form as you typed it in. That means you can just compile the file you printed to. So reading a file of this kind is just:

```
define readthing(filename);
    compile(filename);
enddefine;
```

And presto, your object will be sitting on the top of the stack. For example:

```
: writething([magic presto files], 'myfile.p');
: readthing('myfile.p') -> x;
: x =>
** [magic presto files]
```

The filename was given as with .p on the end because that is convention for compilable POP-11 files. Just to recap – this technique only works when the file you will be making is in compilable form. The procedure **writething** will print absolutely anything, it is reading them back with **compile** that makes the restrictions. The simplest objects which print out that way are lists containing just words, numbers and other lists.

Third problem: reading files on your own. The most primitive method is to build a character repeater, and then call it each time you want a character. One step up, you build an item repeater, and call it for each item you want.

Supposing you've got the file made by **writething** above, you can try this:

```
: vars getter;
: incharitem(discin('myfile.p')) -> getter;
: getter() =>
** [
: getter() =>
** magic
```

and so on. Eventually **getter** will return <termin>, which means you've hit the end of the file. With this, you can read any file into a list of items, like this:

```
define readtolist(filename);
vars getter item;
    incharitem(discin(filename)) -> getter;
    [% until (getter() ->> item) = termin do
            item;
        enduntil %]
enddefine;
```

Be warned, however, that this procedure won't return structures: just a list of items. See the beginning of this chapter for more details.

If you want to get a list of all the characters, just remove the call of incharitem from readtolist.

If you want to make a dynamic list out of all the characters in a file, it is simply:

```
: pdtolist(discin('myfile.p')) -> list;
```


Compiler Procedures

Consider one of the 'factory' procedures described above: they take some form of specification as input, and return a procedure for doing some task according to the specification. It is true that the connections between the input to the factory and the output of the result procedures are relatively straightforward. (Although the itemising can be complex.) However, how would you write such a procedure?

All artificial intelligence languages have a method by which they can execute pieces of themselves which have been written by their own procedures: PROLOG has call/1 and LISP has eval. These take as input structures which could have been made by any method, and operate on them exactly as they do on programs which come to them in the ordinary way.

Compare this with more conventional languages. The classical method is where the source text is made in an editor, sometimes (still) as primitive as a card punch. This is then compiled into a file of assembler code, which is then assembled into object code. Then you link the object code, possibly several files, into an executable image file, which you then ask the operating system to run. When you actually run the program, the compiler, which is the part which understands the source language, is not around any more. In an interpreted system, the part which understands the source is around when your program is running, but typically no provision is made for interpreting program text which has been made by your program. Of course, you can always write it out to a file and run the interpreter on that.

POP-11 has several mechanisms for doing this. The simplest is a procedure called popval:

popval(*LIST*);

Evaluates the argument list as POP-11 source. Any results of the evaluation are left on the stack when popval returns.

The list you give to popval can be *any* POP-11 text whatsoever. For example, you've been shown no way to have your program declare variables whose names aren't decided until your program runs. Now you could write a procedure like this:

```
define declare(name);
    popval([vars ^name;]);
enddefine;
```

Another procedure is available which compiles from character consumers:

compile(*SOURCESPEC*);

Compiles the source specified by the argument. If the argument is a string, it is taken to be the name of a file, which is opened and then compiled. If the argument is a procedure, it is taken to be a character consumer, whose characters are compiled until it returns <termin>. Any results from the compilation are left on the stack when compile returns.

A key feature of POP-11 is that it is incremental: it is either interpreted, or incrementally compiled. This means you can add new structures and procedures at any time, and the compiler is always around to deal with them. All current systems are incrementally compiled, which is why the procedure is called compile, but an interpreted system would behave in exactly the same way. The design philosophy was to give users the flexibility and ease of interaction of an interpretive system, but with the speed of a compiled one.

The Truth About compile

The input mechanisms involved in the compilation process are a little more complicated than presented so far.

Conceptually, the primitive procedure is popval, which compiles from a list. The procedure compile could be written in terms of it, like the code below. You'll see that it sets up cucharin from its argument, and then sets up proglist. This is a dynamic list, which behaves as though it is a list of the entire input stream. You are referred to the section on dynamic lists in the data types chapter. After doing that, it just popvals the proglist.

```
define compile(spec);
vars cucharin proglist;
    if isstring(spec) then
        discin(spec)
    else
        spec
    endif -> cucharin;
    pdtolist(incharitem(cucharin)) -> proglist;
    popval(proglist);
enddefine;
```

Notice that **cucharin** and **proglist** are local to **compile**. This means that, for example, a file could redirect its input to a different place, and after the file was compiled input would come from the original place. You may come across something like this in files:

```
vars hello;
[hello there] -> hello;
[] -> proglist;
hello =>
```

The assignment into **proglist** tells POP-11 that the current input is finished, and it won't compile past there.

If you tried this:

```
: compile('foo.p');
```

you'd get no output from the file, because as far as POP-11 is concerned, the file has ended, because **proglist** is empty. However, the previous portion of the file was compiled correctly, as this testifies:

```
: hello =>
** [hello there]
```

So what does **popval** do? It is defined something like this:

```
define popval(proglist);
    really_really_compile(proglist);
enddefine;
```

And of course, **really_really_compile** really does the work, and would involve a call like **basicplot(termin)**. (A note: **really_really_compile** and **basicplot** don't actually exist, they have just been for explanation. All the other procedures named are real procedures you can use.)

The procedure **readitem** (the one which doesn't expand macros) simply reads items from the head of **proglist**, as shown overleaf:

```
define readitem( );
    if null( proglist) then
        termin
    else
        hd( proglist);
        tl( proglist) -> proglist;
    endif;
enddefine;
```

Because proglist is (usually) a dynamic list, when we need more items than have actually been read so far, the embedded procedure in the dynamic list will be called. If popval had been called by compile, this would be an item repeater based on the current cucharin, and that's where the characters actually come from.

Of course, readitem is normally called by itemread, which looks at the incoming item and if it is a word, decides if it is a macro (by calling identprops) and if it is, expanding it.

Macro expansion is actually quite a simple process. Any word which has identprops macro has its value checked:

Procedures are run, and the results put onto proglist
Contents of lists are put on the front of proglist
Other values are put onto the front of proglist

This is one of the reasons why the compilation is done through lists – we can put any amount of stuff back onto the front of proglist. This is very convenient in a compiler. Also, we can look ahead into the compilation stream, to see if something is coming. This is useful, for example, in the part of the compilation where we have to see if the item after the current one is an opening bracket or not.

itemread could have been written like this:

```
define itemread( );
vars item;
    readitem( ) -> item;
    if isword( item) and identprops( item) == "macro" then
        valof( item) -> item;
        if isprocedure( item) then
            [% item( ) %] <> proglist
        elseif islist( item) then
            item <> proglist
        else
            item :: proglist
        endif -> proglist;
        itemread( )
    else
        item
    endif
enddefine;
```

Actual Executable Code

It may be of interest to some readers to see what kinds of machine instructions are
executed for a piece of POP-11 code. What follows isn't from a real POP-11 system,
but it does give an idea of what the structures look like at the lowest level. It is genuine
68000 assembler output, and shows a plausible method for what the compiler might
make. At the very least, it shows that connection between the rude numbers actually
in the machine, and the source code at the top. Readers unfamiliar or unhappy with
assembler code and hexadecimal numbers are warned off here.

The example is for the **is3** procedure in the worked compilation shown earlier in
this chapter:

```
define is3(thing) -> result;
    thing = 3 -> result;
enddefine;
```

Which makes the following virtual machine code. You'll notice it's slightly different
from that shown earlier. Instead of the two **LOCAL** instructions for **thing** and
result, we have **SAVE** at the beginning, and **RESTORE** at the end. When a variable
is declared local to a procedure, it first makes sure it is declared as a variable, which
happens at compile time. At run time, we save and restore the value of the variable,
as shown here.

```
PROCEDURE
SAVE        "thing"
SAVE        "result"
POP         "thing"

PUSH        "thing"
PUSHQ       3
CALL        "="

POP         "result"

PUSH        "result"
RESTORE     "result"
RESTORE     "thing"
ENDPROCEDURE

-> is3;
```

Structures

In this example, each pointer takes one 'longword': 32 bits. We can distinguish integers from pointers because all the pointers are large (more than FF0000 hex) and all the integers are small (less than this). Negative numbers have been ignored.

Every structure begins with a key, which is an integer. Properly, keys are actually structures, but the idea is that we have a uniform way of deciding what kind of object we are pointing to. So if we have a longword which is large, it is a pointer. The longword which it points to contains an integer, which is small. The integer says what kind of object it is, according to the list of symbols WORD_KEY, PROCEDURE_KEY, and so on.

00000000	WORD_KEY	equ	0
00000001	PROCEDURE_KEY	equ	1
00000002	STRING_KEY	equ	2
00000003	BOOLEAN_KEY	equ	3
00000004	NIL_KEY	equ	4

Each structure has a format. For example, a word consists of four longwords, which contain, respectively, the key, the value, the identprops, and the string containing the characters for the word. Offsets are defined for each of these, from the start of the structure:

00000000	W_KEY	equ	0
00000004	W_VALOF	equ	4
00000008	W_IDENT	equ	8
0000000C	W_STRING	equ	12

Strings consist of a key, a length (in characters) and the characters. The characters are packed into successive bytes, and are padded out to a whole number of longwords. Notice that while a word is always the same size (four longwords), a string is at least two longwords, but may be more – you have to look at the S_LENGTH field to see how long.

00000000	S_KEY	equ	0
00000004	S_LENGTH	equ	4
00000008	S_CHARS	equ	8

A procedure is like a string. It has a key, a length, and then the meat. Of course, in this case the meat is executable code, not characters. But the remarks about the length hold here too.

00000000	PD_KEY	equ	0
00000004	PD_LENGTH	equ	4
00000008	PD_EXCUTE	equ	8

We'll assume that the word for = and all the structures needed for that are defined somewhere else. Let's assume that the word = is at the label equals.

Here we say all the structures start at 'big' addresses. This might be plausible for some 68000 systems somewhere, but it would be unusual.

00FF0000		org	$ ff0000

A couple of primitive structures, just to show them. Special objects would typically be just a key. The only thing you can do with them is compare them against other things, and print them, so there is no need for them to actually have any 'content'.

00FF0000		false:	
00FF0000	00000003	dc.l	BOOLEAN_KEY
00FF0004		nil:	
00FF0004	00000004	dc.l	NIL_KEY

Here's the word **thing**. See that, like all the structures, it begins with a key, and then has its component parts: we have simulated the effect of doing

: vars thing;
: false -> thing;

As you see, this word has identprops 0 and value **false**:

00FF0008		thing:	
00FF0008	00000000	dc.l	WORD_KEY
00FF000C	00FF0000	dc.l	false
00FF0010	00000000	dc.l	0
00FF0014	00FF0038	dc.l	thing_str

result has value **nil** and identprops 0:

00FF0018		result:	
00FF0018	00000000	dc.l	WORD_KEY
00FF001C	00FF0004	dc.l	nil
00FF0020	00000000	dc.l	0
00FF0024	00FF0048	dc.l	result_str

Finally, **is3** has as its value the procedure we defined, and also identprops 0.

00FF0028		is3:	
00FF0028	00000000	dc.l	WORD_KEY
00FF002C	00FF0064	dc.l	is3pdr
00FF0030	00000000	dc.l	0
00FF0034	00FF0058	dc.l	is3_str

As all words print out differently, their characters must be stored somewhere. The usual thing is to have the words point to strings, which we have done. Here are the strings:

```
OOFF0038                    thing_str:
OOFF0038   00000002              dc.l              STRING_KEY
OOFF003C   00000005              dc.l              5
OOFF0040   7468696E              dc.l              'thing'
OOFF0044   67000000

OOFF0048                    result_str:
OOFF0048   00000002              dc.l              STRING_KEY
OOFF004C   00000006              dc.l              6
OOFF0050   72657375              dc.l              'result'
OOFF0054   6C740000

OOFF0058                    is3_str:
OOFF0058   00000002              dc.l              STRING_KEY
OOFF005C   00000003              dc.l              3
OOFF0060   69733300              dc.l              'is3'
```

Finally, the procedure for **is3**. This procedure was 'compiled' (by hand) on the assumption that words never move in memory. Some POP-11 systems arrange this. Also, we have assumed that the POP-11 argument stack is pointed to by register A6.

First, there is some header, which gives the key, as always, and the length:

```
OOFF0064                    is3pdr:
OOFF0064   00000001              dc.l              PROCEDURE_KEY
OOFF0068   0000004A              dc.l              is3pdr_end-is3pdr
```

Then we have the saving of the old values of the local variables on the calling stack. This just involves pushing the values, in the way familiar to every assembler language programmer, and implements the

```
SAVE       "thing"
SAVE       "result"
```

of the VM code:

```
OOFF006C   2F3900FF              move.l            thing+W_VALOF,-(a7)
OOFF0070   000C
OOFF0072   2F3900FF              move.l            result+W_VALOF,-(a7)
OOFF0076   001C
```

After that, we pop our argument from the user stack:

```
POP        "thing"
```

which is the last thing we had to do in our prologue:

```
00FF0078  23DE00FF                    move.l        (a6)+,thing+W_VALOF
00FF007C  000C
```

Next, we had to implement

thing = 3

which turns into

```
PUSH       "thing"
PUSHQ      3
CALL       "="
```

The first move.l pushes the contents of the address, while the second moves the immediate value 3:

```
00FF007E  2D3900FF                    move.l        thing+W_VALOF,-(a6)
00FF0082  000C
00FF0084  2D3C0000                    move.l        #3,-(a6)
00FF0088  0003
```

To implement the CALL virtual machine instruction, we first have to take the value of the word =, which we fetch into register A0:

```
00FF008A  20790123                    move.l        equals+W_VALOF,a0

00FF008E  0004
```

And then we jump to the executable code, which is offset from the register. In a real system, there would normally be a check that A0 pointed to a procedure here.

```
00FF0090  4EA80008                    jsr           PD_EXECUTE(a0)
```

After the CALL, we pop the result into result:

```
00FF0094  23DE00FF                    move.l        (a6)+,result+W_VALOF
00FF0098  001C
```

And at the end of a procedure with output locals, we have to stack them. This procedure just has the single result result:

```
00FF009A  2D3900FF                    move.l        result+W_VALOF,-(a6)
00FF009E  001C
```

At the end of a procedure with local variables, they must restored from the calling stack:

```
OOFFOOAO  23DFOOFF              move.l     (a7)+,thing+W_VALO:
OOFFOOA4  OOOC
OOFFOOA6  23DFOOFF              move.l     (a7)+,result+W_VALO
OOFFOOAA  OO1C
```

And finally, we return to the calling procedure:

```
OOFFOOAC  4E75                  rts
OOFFOOAE              is3pdr_end:
```

Optimisations

You may have noticed cases where we could have made better code in this example: quite so, and most compilers do. As well as the usual business about optimising different kinds of branches, a POP followed by a PUSH (as done with thing) and a PUSH followed by a POP (as done with result) are often optimised.

CHAPTER 12

Fancy Procedures and Control Structures

Introduction

We have already covered the basics of procedures and control structures. It must be said that other kinds of procedure are rarely used, but can be invaluable. The same goes for the non-standard control structures which POP-11 provides. This chapter covers the more unusual features, for those occasional needs.

Recursion

(Readers familiar with this topic are advised to skip to the next section.)

Recursion isn't a fancy control structure: it is covered here for completeness and because you must have a good grasp of it for many of the topics in this chapter. In common with most modern programming languages, a great many POP-11 procedures are recursive, which is to say that they call themselves. Many of the procedures in this book have been recursive.

If you are unfamiliar with this concept, think about how POP-11 prints objects such as lists. These are often nested, like this:

[[this is a list] inside another list]

To print the outer list, POP-11 has to print an opening square bracket, then the elements of the list, then the closing bracket. Notice that in this description, there is nothing about what kind of objects the elements are: and as we have seen, they are often lists themselves.

To make this work, there must be a primitive procedure for printing objects such as words, strings and numbers (let's call this **printprimitive**). Then the main printing procedure would look something like the code overleaf:

Notice how closely it corresponds to the English description: lists are printed item by item, with brackets around them. Other items (assumed to be 'primitive') are just printed directly. (Note: the actual printing procedure **pr** is very much like this, except more complicated, because it must deal with many data types, and because its primitive procedure is actually **cucharout**, which prints single characters.)

```
define print(item);
vars subitem;
    if islist(item) then
        printprimitive('[');
        for subitem in item do
            print(subitem);
            printprimitive(' ');
        endfor;
        printprimitive(']');
    else
        printprimitive(item);
    endif;
enddefine;
```

How does this work? If you haven't come across recursion before, it will probably look like magic, but it isn't. The trick is to look at the structures of the list. While we don't know how deeply the list might be nested, we do know that it is finite. That is, at some point, the lists won't have any more lists as elements. At that point, the recursion 'bottoms out', because the invocations of print will all call printprimitive. Notice that the empty list will also end the recursion.

We know that the lists will be finitely nested because we have no way of making any other kind. Imagine that, when the POP-11 system starts up, there are no lists other than the empty list. Then, the first list is made: it can't have any (non-empty) lists as elements, as there aren't lists to build it from. The second list made might have the first as one of its elements, giving it a nesting of one. And so on: the deepest the 100th list might be is 99. (It might strike you that inductive proofs like this are recursive too: maths teachers have the same concepts to get across.)

So, because we can't take lists apart and forever find more lists, the procedure print above will always terminate, given time. All recursive procedures work on the principle of having a 'terminating case', and reduce their problem, eventually, to a simple solution which can be dealt with by a different procedure.

The particular language feature which allows POP-11 to have recursive procedures is the local variable. Many novice programmers have felt that the different invocations of the same procedure ought to interfere with each other. In print, for example, why don't the local variables item and subitem get messed up? The answer is that each invocation of print stores the old values away, and restores them when it is done. This is described in previous chapters.

Now here's the truth: it is possible to make structures which go on forever, and if you give them to the printarrow, it will print forever. Such structures are called circular, as they contain pointers to themselves. A small one might look like that shown in Figure 12.1. You can make these structures because the procedures for accessing parts of structures also have updaters, so you can write:

```
: [hello there] -> x;
: 3 -> hd(x);
: x =>
** [3 there]
```

Fig. 12.1

You can make a circular list like this:

```
: [1] -> x;
: x -> tl(x);
```

but if you tried to print it out, you would get this:

```
** [1 1 1 1 1 1 1 1 1 1 1 1 1 1 1 1 1 1 1 1 1 1 1 1 1 1 1 1 1 1 1 1 1
1 1 1 1 1 1 1 1 1 1 1
```

and it would go on until you interrupted your system. The manipulations behind building (and controlling) such structures can be very intricate, and their use is not at all recommended for beginners.

The Calling Stack

As mentioned early in this book, POP-11 has two stacks. The first is the ordinary 'user' stack. The second is the 'calling' stack, which is the place where calling order is recorded, that is, where POP-11 writes down what to continue doing after it is finished with the current procedure.

It was said that there is no way to manipulate the calling stack directly, but this isn't actually true. This section describes the facilities available.

Consider this example: **huey, duey** and **luey** each have a local variable of the same name, and the last can be called by either of the first:

luey finds out which procedure to return to (and where exactly in the procedure) in the usual way, that is, by getting a return address from the calling stack. (Readers interested in the details are directed to any book on assembler programming.)

```
define huey();
vars x;
    3 -> x;
    luey();
    x =>
enddefine;
```

```
define duey();
vars x;
    4 -> x;
    luey();
    x =>
    5 -> x;
    luey();
    x =>
enddefine;

define luey();
vars x;
    6 -> x;
enddefine;
```

The old values of the local variables are also stored on the calling stack, along with other information which POP-11 needs for its housekeeping.

Suppose luey had to find out what procedure called it. We modify it like this:

```
define luey();
vars x;
    6 -> x;
    caller(1) =>
enddefine;
```

And then suppose we call huey:

```
: huey();
** <procedure huey>
** 3
```

English is not a good language for describing what happened: caller returned the procedure which called the caller of the procedure caller.

To make sense of the relationship between the argument to caller and its result, here's another scenario: imagine five procedures called four, three, two, one, and zero, like this:

```
define four(n);     vars n; three(n); enddefine;
define three(n);    vars n; two(n); enddefine;
define two(n);      vars n; one(n); enddefine;
define one(n);      vars n; zero(n); enddefine;
define zero(n);     vars n; caller(n) enddefine;
```

If you try it:

```
: four(3) =>
** <procedure three>
```

you will see that each procedure here is named by how far away it is from the invocation of **caller**.

In the example, at the point where **caller** was doing its work, the calling chain would look like this:

```
setpop
(many system procedures here)
four
three
two
one
zero
caller
```

At the beginning of the calling chain there is always a call to the procedure **setpop**. After that there will be many procedures; those responsible for reading your input and so on, and then your procedures. At any moment, the bottom-most procedure (as shown here) will be the procedure currently executing.

Suppose there were ten system procedures at the mark in the chain: and you ran

```
: four(15) =>
** <procedure setpop>
: four(16) =>
** <false>
```

What you will find is that, according to **caller**, above the **setpop** are an endless series of <false> objects. This enables programs to find out how many procedures are in the calling chain, and examine the current state of program flow.

caller(*CALLER_NUMBER*) -> *PDR*;

This procedure returns the procedure which is *CALLER_NUMBER* procedure calls above the caller of **caller**. That is, the procedure which invokes **caller** has number 0. If there is no such procedure, because the calling chain is not that deep, the result will be <false>. If *CALLER_NUMBER* is not an integer, negative, or not a number, **caller** will cause a mishap.

The Procedure apply

As procedures are first-class data objects in POP-11, there is a full suite of procedures for manipulating them. The principal action you can perform on procedures is applying them – the ordinary procedure application, or invocation.

Of course, this has special syntax in POP-11, the round brackets. However, there is a procedure which has the same action, called **apply**. This applies its argument in the usual way. **apply** could have been written like this:

```
define apply(item);
    item();
enddefine;
```

apply will work on any object, but is mostly used for procedures. Its meaning is really the same as the 'application brackets', and so you can use it to subscript lists, and vectors, and so on. Its main use is for passing as an argument to other procedures, or to keep in data objects.

In POP-11 programs it is quite common for information to be passed between procedures or stored in data structures in varying ways, depending on what it is. For example, you might have two-element lists, where the first element is a procedure to be applied to the second in order to get the needed piece of information.

The following is a rather contrived example of this kind of programming. We have the **getinfo** procedure, which digs out the information, and several of these two-element lists, each of which will produce the number 3 as their information:

```
define getinfo(list);
vars pdr arg;
    list(1) -> pdr;
    list(2) -> arg;
    pdr(arg);
enddefine;

define plus1(x);
    x + 1;
enddefine;
: getinfo([ ^hd [3]] =>
** 3
: getinfo([ ^plus1 2]) =>
** 3
: getinfo([ ^apply ^givethree]) =>
** 3
: getinfo([ ^identfn 3]) =>
** 3
: getinfo([[0 1 2 3 4] 4]) =>
** 3
```

A note on **apply** and arguments. If you are passing arguments to the procedure which **apply** will invoke, they should already be on the stack when **apply** is called, like this:

```
apply(a, b, c, pdr);
```

which has the same action as

```
pdr(a, b, c);
```

apply(*ITEM*);
This procedure applies its argument in the usual way.

Chaining

From the discussion of the calling stack, you should be aware that every procedure invocation takes up some memory – the 'stack frame' – required to be able to reconstruct the environment of the procedure's caller. This includes the local variable values, and a pointer into the caller, saying where to continue when the current procedure is finished.

There are some occasions where this information isn't needed. One is the case when a procedure doesn't do anything after the call to some other procedure. Consider this case:

```
define foo(x);
    x =>
    goo();
enddefine;
```

Here, foo does some work (the printing of x) and then calls goo. After goo returns, foo doesn't do anything. This is a case where foo's stack frame isn't needed. POP-11 has a procedure called chain, which is similar to apply, except that it recovers the stack frame of its caller. This means that when the chained procedure returns, it doesn't return into the chaining procedure, but in the caller of the chaining procedure. The chained procedure takes the place of the chaining one in the stack. Consider this example:

```
define daughter();
    [daughter] =>
enddefine;

define mother();
    [mother 1] =>
    chain(daughter);
    [mother 2] =>
enddefine;
```

```
define grandmother();
    [grandma 1] =>
    mother();
    [grandma 2] =>
enddefine;
```

Here, grandmother calls mother, which chains to daughter, which replaces mother in the stack. So when daughter returns, control is back to grandmother, and the remaining work in mother is lost.

```
: grandmother();
** [grandma 1]
** [mother 1]
** [daughter]
** [grandma 2]
```

Note that while chain looks like an ordinary procedure, its behaviour is quite different. One point of difference is that it doesn't occur in the calling stack. So if daughter were to call caller(1) the result would be grandmother. It wouldn't be mother, because mother chained to daughter. And it wouldn't be chain because chain doesn't leave any evidence.

The uses of chain are rather specialised – treat it with caution. They are mainly to do with error recovery or unusual control requirements, or where stack space has to be very carefully controlled. It is not usually worth chaining to the last procedure in procedure definitions: it makes the code harder to read, and can introduce obscure bugs.

As well as altering the control flow, chain gives the chained procedure a different environment. This is because as the chaining procedure is being left, all of its local variables are restored to their previous values before the chained procedure is started:

```
define showx();
    x =>
enddefine;
```

```
define iki();
vars x;
    3 -> x;
    chain(showx);
enddefine;
```

```
define kik( );
vars x;
    3 -> x;
    showx( );
enddefine;

: 100 -> x;
: iki( );
** 100
: kik( );
** 3
```

You will see that when chained to by iki, showx is run in the enronment which iki was called in, with x holding value 100. But when applied by kik in the normal way, showx gets kik's environment, with x as 3. The comment above about treating chain with respect is underlined by this example.

chain(*ITEM*);

    chain unwinds its caller's stack frame, restoring any local variables, and then calls *ITEM* in its place.

Fancy Chaining Procedures

We have seen chain, which 'loses' the current procedure from the calling stack, and replaces it with the chained procedure. There are four other procedures like chain, which lose procedures from the calling stack: chainto, chainfrom, exitto, and exitfrom.

    exitfrom is a bit like return, except it takes an argument, the procedure to exit from. Remember how return made the current procedure finish immediately; exitfrom makes one of the callers of the current procedure finish immediately.

    Imagine an alphabet of procedures defined like this:

```
define a( );
    pr('a');
    b( );
    pr('a');
enddefine;
```

All the others are the same, except for z:

```
define z( );
    pr('z*');
    pr('z');
enddefine;
```

If we run this, we should get the alphabet, first forwards, then backwards, with a star in between. Suppose we change z to cause an exit from g, like this:

```
define z();
    pr('z*');
    exitfrom(g);
    pr('z');
enddefine;
```

What happens now? Well, everything is the same until we get to z, so we get the alphabet printed out forwards. Then z makes an exit from g, losing the calling stack in between. g is now finished, not having had the chance to print its name a second time, and control is back in f, so we get:

```
: a();
abcdefghijklmnopqrstuvwxyz*fedcba
```

If z makes an exit *to* g, then g will continue, and we get:

```
: a();
abcdefghijklmnopqrstuvwxyz*gfedcba
```

The other two procedures, **chainto** and **chainfrom**, are like their exiting counterparts, but with a **chain** on the end. Another change to z, and another procedure:

```
define boo();
    pr('!boo!');
enddefine;

define z();
    pr('z*');
    chainfrom(g, boo);
    pr('z');
enddefine;
```

Just from the naming it should be easy to guess what happens: alphabet, star, then we leave g, and replace that with boo, which will return into g's caller (which happens to be f):

```
: a();
abcdefghijklmnopqrstuvwxyz*!boo!fedcba
```

And finally, if the **chainfrom** was replaced by a **chainto**, the target procedure is continued, which in this example means we get the second letter 'g'.

The main uses of these kinds of procedure is in error-recovery. For example, imagine a top level procedure like this:

```
define toplevel();
    while dowork(getinput()) do
        [thank you] =>
    endwhile;
enddefine;
```

Any procedure involved in this program could then recover from errors like this:

```
if errorcondition() then
    chainfrom(dowork, error_recover);
endif;
```

Assuming, of course, error_recover was a procedure which could fix up the problem, or perhaps report it to the user.

When using any of the procedures which unwind the calling stack, be warned that they always work with the first instance of the target procedure they find on the way up – which will be the last-called one. This is especially important if the target procedure is recursive. The usual trick is to make such procedures know how deeply nested they are, or to wrap one of them in some other procedure, which won't be called again.

exitto(*TARGET*);

Unwinds the control stack until an invocation of *TARGET* is found, which is then resumed, just as though the procedure it called had returned. Causes a mishap if the argument isn't a procedure, or isn't in the calling stack.

exitfrom(*TARGET*);

Unwinds the control stack until an invocation of *TARGET* is found, which is then exited just as though the target procedure had finished normally. Causes a mishap if the argument isn't a procedure, or isn't in the calling stack.

chainto(*TARGET*, *CHAINEE*);

Unwinds the control stack until an invocation of *TARGET* is found, and replaces the procedure it called with the *CHAINEE* procedure. The *CHAINEE* procedure will return to the *TARGET* when it finishes. Both arguments must be procedures, and *TARGET* must be in the calling stack.

chainfrom(*TARGET*, *CHAINEE*);

Unwinds the control stack until an invocation of *TARGET* is found, which is replaced by the *CHAINEE* procedure. Both arguments must be procedures, and *TARGET* must be in the calling stack.

Closures and Functional Composition

Of all the POP-11 data structures, one of the most useful is also one of the most useless-looking. Closures are simply procedures which have some or all of the arguments locked in at a time before they are run. For this reason, building closures is sometimes called partial application.

There are several major uses – to make general procedures more specific, and to make different procedures uniformly callable, to evaluate arguments in a different context to which the procedure is run, or to delay execution of procedures until needed.

A very simple example of the first is a procedure to print a space, built from the procedure to print ordinary things:

```
: vars prspace;
: pr(% ' ' %) -> prspace;
```

The special syntax is very similar to the normal application brackets, but with percent signs inside. All the arguments are evaluated in the normal way, but then instead of calling the procedure immediately on them, the procedure and the now evaluated arguments are frozen into a single unit, the closure, which remains on the stack. In the example above the closure is then assigned the variable **prspace**.

When the closure is executed, all of the frozen values are put on the stack and the procedure is called.

A closure, then, has a 'procedure part', and a number of 'frozen values'.

As an example of making procedures uniformly callable, consider the example of two-element lists shown in the description of **apply** earlier in this chapter. What was really needed there were closures. We could make a list of closures like this:

```
: vars threes;
: [% hd(% [3] %), plus1(% 2 %), givethree, identfn(% 3 %) %]
:      -> threes;
```

Each element of this list is a procedure; each except the third is a closure; and each, when applied with no arguments, would return the result 3.

Don't confuse the decorated list brackets with the decorated application brackets. The percent signs by the square brackets build the list, while the percent signs by the round brackets build the closures.

The closures shown so far have all had only one argument each, which is the number their procedure-parts needed. If you make closures out of procedures which need more arguments than you have frozen in, the frozen-in values are the rightmost arguments to the procedure. So if you have a procedure

```
define foo(a, b, c);
    a =>
    b =>
    c =>
enddefine;
```

and you make a closure like this:

```
: vars clos;
: foo(% 1, 2 %) -> clos;
```

then the closure clos supplies two arguments (1 and 2) to the procedure foo, which will therefore be expecting another one. When run, foo's argument b will have value 1, and c will be 2. The extra argument will be bound to a:

```
: clos([hello]);
** [hello]
** 1
** 2
```

The closure runs much as if it was defined like this:

```
define clos( );
    1, 2,
    chain(foo);
enddefine;
```

The arguments listed between the percent signs are evaluated at the time of building the closure, while the procedure part of the closure is run when the closure is run. So in this example, look at the values which confuse prints out:

```
define confuse(thawed, frozen);
    thawed =>
    frozen =>
    x =>
enddefine;
```

```
: vars x;
: [a list] -> x;
: vars clos;
: confuse(% x %) -> clos;
: 100 -> x;
: clos(x + 10);
** 110
** [a list]
** 100
```

When clos was built, x had [a list] as its value. So the frozen value of the closure is the list [a list]. Then when it was run, it was passed another argument, which was evaluated to be 110. clos pushes its frozen value, [a list], and then calls its procedure part confuse, which pops its two arguments, prints them, and then prints the value of x, which is 100, the value it was last given.

As with most things which have special syntax, there is also a procedure to perform the same action: **partapply**.

partapply(*PDR, FROZLIST*) -> *CLOSURE*;

Builds a closure out of its two arguments. *PDR* **must be a procedure, and** *FROZLIST* **can be a list of any length.**

Getting at the Closure's Components

Given a closure, you can find out what its frozen values are, and what the procedure part is.

If *c* evaluates to a closure:

pdpart(*c*)   returns the procedure part of the closure.

frozval(*N, c*)   returns the *N*th frozen value of the closure. The leftmost frozen value is numbered 1. If *N* is more than the highest-numbered frozen value, a mishap is generated.

datalength(*c*)   returns the number of frozen values of the closure.

datalist(*c*)   returns a list of all the frozen values of the closure.

Both **frozval** and **pdpart** have updaters, so you can change the frozen values and procedure parts of closures. Neither action is recommended.

Procedure Composition

The procedures on data structures introduced the append operator <>, which joined any two objects of the same type. It also works for procedures. This is not the greatest of POP-11's tools, but it can make life a little easier.

Suppose we have two procedures called **addl** and **times2**, which each take a single numeric argument and produce obvious results:

```
: vars addltimes2;
: addl <> times2 -> addltimes2;
: addltimes2(3) =>
** 8
```

Procedure Syntax

Perhaps 99 percent of the procedures most POP-11 programmers write are of the ordinary kind presented so far in this book. The remaining one percent are operators, macros, and syntax words. Some people, including this author, believe that such facilities are over-used, and make programs harder to read and less likely to work. Many of the same people, including this author again, believe in giving people the rope to use as they will. However, for most programmers, both macros and syntax words are of relatively little use, compared with the effort of learning to use them. As most of that effort is beyond the scope of this book, they are not presented beyond the following description of what they are.

Most identifiers behave as you have seen them do throughout this book. Mentioning their name either pushes their value onto the stack, or if followed by application brackets, applies their value:

```
: length =>
** <procedure length>
: length('hello') =>
** 5
```

The example shows that the value of the word **length** is some procedure, and following the word by round brackets applies the procedure, in this case to the string 'hello'.

We have also seen the procedures **identprops** and **valof** both of which act on words. The first returns a value indicating if the word is an identifer, and if so, what kind. The second returns the value of an identifier.

```
: identprops("length") =>
** 0
: valof("length") =>
** <procedure length>
```

Here we see that the word **length** is the name of an identifier, which has code zero. This indicates that the identifier is of the ordinary variety. Then we see that value is the procedure we saw earlier.

The fancier kinds of procedure, so-called, are actually exactly the same kinds of procedure. The difference is in the syntactic qualities of the identifier of which they are the value. When we speak of the operator **matches**, the only thing which makes it an operator is the identprops of the word **matches**. The procedure in the value of identifier **matches** is no different at all.

Operators are the same as ordinary identifiers, except they sit between their arguments. We have come across these in the shape of the operator **matches**, as well as the host of arithmetic operators.

Macros are more common. They can shorten your programs significantly, and make them clearer, if used judiciously. There are few macros built-in to POP-11, although the printarrow, **recordclass** and **vectorclass** are sometimes implemented as macros.

Syntax words are for when you need to add new keywords to POP-11 for some purpose. The main place this finds use is where some action in your program is extremely common, and unclear in plain POP-11. This book treats these no further, as writing them normally necessitates intimate details of the system. Be warned: portability can be a problem with syntax words.

Review

Before continuing with the other procedure types, a review of syntax of the ordinary type is in order.

Because of the evolution of POP-11, other syntaxes may be allowed by your system. In particular, most of the older POP-2 syntax still works on many systems. However, none of it has been presented in this book, and you are recommended only to use the syntax shown here, as future systems may not be upward compatible with the older ones.

It consists of

define	Introduces a new procedure definition
NAME	The name you want for this procedure
(	Introduces the argument names
ARGNAMES	The names you want for the arguments. If there is more than one, separate them with commas.
)	Marks the end of the argument names.
-> *RESNAME*	Marks first result variable. Repeat as desired, or omit if no result variables.
;	Marks end of definition header.

Operators

The definition of an operator is exactly like the definition of an ordinary procedure, except that a number is inserted immediately after the keyword **define**, and writing the operator in normal prefix notation. This number is the precedence of the operator. Operators with lower precedence are tighter-binding. Positive precedences associate to the left, while negative associate to the right. There are no right-associative operators built in to POP-11, and your implementation may not support them.

Associativity is the property of the operator which decides how to interpret an expression like this:

: 1 - 2 - 3 =>

The question arises because the subtraction operator - can only deal with two numbers at a time. A left-associative (that is, normal) operator groups the subexpressions on the left, making the previous expression exactly the same as

: (1 - 2) - 3 =>
** -4

This is easy to remember because it is just the same old left-to-right evaluation that POP-11 always does.

If – were right-associative (that is, abnormal for POP-11), then the expression without brackets would be the same as

```
: 1 - (2 - 3) =>
** 2
```

You can also declare operator variables without defining a procedure to put in their value, by putting a precedence number after the **vars** keyword.

Because operators don't need brackets to show that they are being applied, special syntax is needed to show when they aren't being applied. Every time you want to mention an operator, in order to take its value, you need to temporarily switch off its operator status, by putting the word **nonop** in front of it:

```
: nonop matches =>
** <procedure matches>
```

Examples

An operator to do 'cons onto list unless present', such as might be used in set manipulations:

```
define 7 ::_?(item, list);
    if member(item, list) then
        list
    else
        item :: list
    endif;
enddefine;
```

An operator variable, with the procedure **member** in it:

```
: vars 7 elementof;
: member -> nonop elementof;
: 3 elementof [1 2 3 4 5] =>
** <true>
```

Because the declaration of **elementof** was as an operator of precedence 7, we can't write

```
: member -> elementof;
```

so we use the **nonop** syntax.

Precedence

An expression such as 1 + 2 * 3 is, in itself, ambiguous. The method we use to disambiguate it is to give each operator a precedence, and group them in that order.

The **+** operator has precedence 5, while * has precedence 4; and as the expression is grouped in precedence order, the * has first go, and so the expression is equivalent to 1 + (2 * 3), and not with the brackets around the 1 and the 2.

Precedence Numbers

In POP-11, precedence numbers range from -12.8 to 12.7 inclusive, and there may be an implementation dependent limit to the resolution you can use. The ranges for all known POP-11 systems are either the integers 1 to 12 (no right associativity), or the 255 values –12.8 to 12.7, in tenths, excluding 0.

Afterword

After the rigours of the previous chapters, a little reflection is called for.

It is hoped that you have enjoyed working with POP-11 as much as this author has. It is true to say that it is a language which has spoilt many people for programming in the more common languages.

As described in the introduction, POP-11 was developed as a language for artificial intelligence work. But it is coming to be used in many other areas as well. The arguments in favour of this are strong. If programming is not your main interest, you want to spend less time learning about computers and more time dealing with fluid dynamics, or carpet design, or whatever. A language like POP-11 helps you to do this by letting you bring powerful data structures and flexibility to play in every line of code you write.

If programming is your main interest, learning more and different languages strengthens the basic tools of your trade: thinking of ways of representing objects and ways of manipulating those representations. Every language suggests new ways of doing things. Especially notable are the cleanliness of passing procedures around, and putting them in data structures; the range of data structures available; and the clarity and simplicity of the syntax.

Many people have learnt POP-11 as their first programming language, psychologists and philosophers among them. It may help to break the myth that all programming is about numerical subjects, and arithmetic fluency is a prerequisite for programming. Indeed, such classical subjects as compiler writing are far better suited to symbolic processing languages than older numerically-bound ones.

Those who will go on to learn other languages may have some rude shocks coming. However, they may have an easier time of it than people learning POP-11 after many years of PASCAL and C, because they may have to unlearn a lot of techniques which quite simply aren't applicable.

It is true that most of these comments apply to other artificial intelligence languages such as LISP, PROLOG and SMALLTALK. Even so, there are features of POP-11 which make it stand out even amongst this elite. It isn't that these languages are especially impoverished. Instead, it is more the collection of little features which make up your day at the terminal.

The intention here is not to suggest that POP-11 is a cure for the common cold. Far from it. For many good reasons, people write programs in many different languages. Issues to do with availability, environment, licensing, cost, speed, and interfacing all play in the tradeoffs. However, in a great number of programming tasks, the single

197

most important (and hence costly) resource is programmer time. Any language which reduces the amount of time a programmer wastes reimplementing the wheel or waiting for programs to compile may be worth any inconveniences it has.

On the negative side, POP-11 suffers most from availability and environmental aspects. There are only a handful of implementations, and relatively few able POP-11 programmers. These things will change as the implementations become available for cheaper machines, in turn producing programmers from schools, colleges and universities. Hopefully, this book and others will help spread the expertise, along with the user groups and bulletin boards.

All current implementations are highly interactive, because of the uses they have been designed for. Many programming tasks require that their end result is a standalone program which can be distributed in executable form for licensing reasons. Implementations which fit this bill will come as the demand rises.

An appendix gives names and addresses of contacts for various POP-11 resources, and a bibliography.

Answers and Hints to Exercises

Exercises 2A

1. (a) ** bonjour
   (b) ** hercule
   (c) MISHAP: SUBSCRIPT OUT OF RANGE
       INVOLVING: [bonjour monsieur poirot] 10

2. (a) : hello(2) =>
   (b) : goodbye(1) =>
   (c) : goodbye(7) =>

Exercises 2B

1. (a) ** [canary peacock]
   (b) ** dalmation
   (c) ** peacock
   (d) ** []

2. (a) : hd(tl(birds)) =>
   (b) : tl(dogs) =>
   (c) : tl(tl(tl(birds))) => or
       : tl(tl(tl(dogs))) =>
   (d) : tl(tl(birds)) =>

3. (a) ** determiner
   (b) ** verbphrase

4. (a) : hd(tl(hd(tl(tl(tl(hd(tl(parse)))))))) =>
   (b) : tl(hd(tl(hd(tl(tl(parse)))))) =>

Exercises 2C

1. (a) ** [[a b c] x y]
   (b) ** [a b c [x y]]
   (c) ** [a b c x y]

    (d) ** [[a b c] [x y] []]
    (e) ** [[a b c] [a b c]]
    (f) ** [a b c iguana [[]] aardvark]

2. (a) : [^^bad ^^good] =>
    (b) : [^ugly ^bad ^good] =>
    (c) : [[^bad]] =>
    (d) : [[^good] ^bad ^^bad] =>
    (e) : good =>
    also
       : [^^good] =>
    (f) : [^^good d e f g] =>

Exercises 3

1. (a) [= = =]
    (b) [= middle =]
    (c) [= second ==]
    (d) [hello == goodbye]
    (e) [= == interim == =]
    (f) [i == mother ==]

2. (a) All lists which end with [], e.g. [hello []] and [[]].
    (b) All lists which have a single item which is a list, e.g.
[[]] and [[watson please come here i want you]]
    (c) All two-element lists which begin with noun, e.g.
[noun [another lexical category]] and [noun noun].
    (d) All lists which begin with noun, e.g. [noun] and
[noun with lots of other things].
    (e) There aren't two examples: only the two-element list consisting of noun and
then dog: [noun dog].

3. Any list which doesn't contain a list or the word noun, or some more difficult
ones: [dog noun] and [[] [[]]].
4. The most you can match is three: [noun dog] matches c, d and e; [noun []]
matchs a, c and d.

Exercises 4A

1. (a) ** <undef dog>
    (b) ** [uno]

(c) ** []
(d) ** [uno]
(e) ** []
(f) ** []

2. ** [katze]   by ein
    ** [kitty]   by zwei
    ** [kitty]   by drei
    ** [kitty]   by vier
    ** \<undef cat\>   from the top level

Exercise 4B

SAVE	"item", "wanted"
POP	"wanted"
POP	"item"
PUSH	"item"
PUSH	"wanted"
CALL	"::"
RESTORE	"item", "wanted"

Exercises 4C

1. These definitions are by no means the only way to do these procedures. If yours
works, well done.

   (a) define addback(obj, list) -> newlist;
         list [^^list ^obj] -> newlist;
      enddefine;

   (b) define addboth(item, list) -> pushmepullu;
         [^item ^^list ^item] -> pushmepullu;
      enddefine;

   (c) define setadd(element, set) -> result;
         element :: delete(element, set) -> result;
      enddefine;

   (d) define double(somelist);
         somelist <> somelist;
      enddefine;

(e) define twin(thing);
       [ˆthing ˆthing];
     enddefine

(f) define setremove(element, set) -> newset;
       delete(element, set) -> newset;
     enddefine;

(g) define addlen(somelist);
       length(somelist) :: somelist;
     enddefine;

2. As with any English description of a program, two people never write exactly the same thing. Just compare the gists.

(a) Takes any object, and returns a one-element list containing that object.

(b) Takes two objects, and returns a three-element list which begins with the word nounphrase, then its two arguments in order. It is designed for making lists which represent the parsetrees of noun phrases, as illustrated in a previous chapter.

(c) Takes an object, and returns a boolean result indicating if the object is in the correct format to represent a noun phrase parsetree, according to the scheme illustrated in a previous chapter: a three-element list beginning with nounphrase and followed by two lists.

(d) Takes a list, and returns a copy of it but without any instances of the word dog.

(e) Exactly the same as nodogs1.

(f) Takes a list, and *prints* a copy of it without any instances of dog in it.

If you are confused about the difference between nodogs1 and nodogs3, try defining them and then trying these:

    : nodogs1([cat dog bat]) =>
    : nodogs3([cat dog bat]) =>

Exercises 5A

1. (a) ** [2 3]
    (b) ** [2 3]
    (c) ** <false>
    (d) ** [3]

(e) ** [cat]

(f) ** [[2]]

2.   Different answer for c. q2 returns [] instead of <false>.

3.   q2 behaves exactly like q1 except that q2 returns [] where q1 returns <false>. So to make q3, copy q2 and add this just before the **enddefine**:

```
if aa = [] then
    false -> aa;
endif;
```

4.   There are always two calls. q2 and q3 first call **member** with their second argument and the third, then the first and the third. q1 makes its calls the other way, so for

```
: q1([2], [3], [[2] 3 1]) =>
```

it first does

```
member([2], [[2] 3 1]) and the result is <true>
```

and then

```
member([3], [[2] 3 1]) and the result is <false>
```

5.   Of course, this is a matter of taste. Unless the 'find-neither' result must be <false>, q2 is probably best. It is the shortest, the most easily extensible, and has a simple interpretation: 'which of these two things can you find in this list?'

6.   This is one way:

```
define italianfor(english) -> italian;
    if english = [small black coffee] then
        [espresso] -> italian;
    else
        false -> italian;
    endif;
enddefine;
```

7.   This is another:

```
define italianfor(english);
    if english = [small black coffee] then
        [espresso]
    elseif english = [large white coffee] then
        [cappuccino]
    else
        [parli inglese]
    endif;
enddefine;
```

8.   Both the two versions of **italianfor** above do 'sensible' things if they don't recognise the input. The crucial thing is to have an **else** clause. The <false> result is probably best if the result is to be used by another procedure. If the result is to be spoken by a human, the second is probably better.

Exercises 5B

1.   Iterative:

```
define addup1(list) -> total;
vars element;
    0 -> total;
    for element in list do
        element + total -> total;
    endfor;
enddefine;
```

Recursive:

```
define addup2(list);
    if list = [] then
        0;
    else
        hd(list) + addup2(tl(list));
    endif;
enddefine;
```

Another recursive one:

```
define addup3(list);
    if list = [] then
        0;
    else
        addup3(tl(list)) + hd(list);
    endif;
enddefine;
```

What's the difference in execution of **addup2** and **addup3**? Consider what would happen if you had subtraction instead of addition. Why might the first be called breadth-first and the second depth-first?

2.   The only way to do this is recursively:

```
define anymem1(item, tree);
    if tree = [] then
        false;
    elseif item = tree then
        true;
    else
        anymem1(hd(tree)) or anymem1(tl(tree));
    endif;
enddefine;
```

Again, consider what would happen if you swapped the order of the recursive calls. Which is depth-first and which is breadth-first? As you can see, tree-searching is easy recursively. For those who are fanatical about minimising recursion, here's a mixed approach:

```
define anymem2(item, tree);
vars subtree;
    for subtree in tree do
        if item = subtree then
            return(true);
        elseif islist(subtree) then
            if anymem2(item, subtree) then
                return(true);
            endif;
        endif;
    endfor;
    false;
enddefine;
```

In practice, **anymem2** will probably be faster than **anymem1**. How great the difference will be depends on whether your system is an interpreter or a compiler. Whether the extra complexity is worth it depends on whether your time spent programming is more valuable than computer time.

A full warpaint version might look like this:

```
define anymembest(item, tree);
vars subtree;
    if islist(tree) then
        for subtree in tree do
            if anymembest(item, subtree) then
                return(true);
            endif;
        endfor;
    else
        item = tree;
    endif;
enddefine;
```

There are some subtle differences in the behaviour between this version and the previous ones: what are they? (Hint: think about different kinds of arguments.)

3. The 'best' version:

```
define addnested(tree);
vars subtree total;
    0 -> total;
    if islist(tree) then
        for subtree in tree do
            addnested(subtree) + total -> total;
        endfor;
    else
        tree -> total;
    endif;
enddefine;
```

Exercises 6

The exercises are intended to be open-ended: there are no answers.

1.  ```
    define subst(old, new, list);
    vars item;
        [% for item in list do
            if item = old then
                new
            else
                item
            endif;
          endfor;
        %]
    enddefine;
    ```

2. Read Chapter 5 again.

3.  ```
    define countlists(list) -> total;
    vars item total;
        0 -> total;
        for item in list do
            if islist(item) then
                total + 1 -> total;
            endif;
        endfor;
    enddefine;
    ```

4. The question here is what do you do to each word to get the numbers. You get 3 if each word is 'worth' 0, you get 10 if a word is worth its length, you get 9 if every object is worth the number of characters it takes to print it. You get 6 if you understand German.

5.
```
define fac(n);
    if n <= 0 then
        1;
    else
        fac(n - 1) * n;
    endif;
enddefine;
```

Many other versions possible, like this one:
```
define fac(n) -> total;
vars i total;
    1 -> total;
    for i from 1 to n do
        total * i -> total;
    endfor;
enddefine;
```

Your system may have bigintegers: in which case there won't be a largest number.

6. Think about a structure like this:

[[dog chien] [cat chat] [breakfast petit_dejuner]]

7. Look at addup of the previous chapter, and remember the procedure length.

8. The trick is to reduce the problem from sorting a big list into comparing objects two at a time. There are hundreds of sorting algorithms: any conventional computer science text will help you here.

9. Use member a lot.

10. Try using matches. To go from millimetres to inches you divide by 25.4.

Exercises 7

1.
```
define glue(left, right);
    [% left, right %];
enddefine;
```

The second one would be

```
define gluetails(left, right) -> glued;
    [% tl(left), tl(right) %] glued;
enddefine;
```

2. (a) The -> should be a ->>. Because if it isn't, if you run it you will get a mishap because the stack will be empty. Also, it doesn't work on the empty list.

(b) It stacks all the tails of a list. There are as many tails as there are items. This procedure doesn't work on empty lists: why?

(c)
```
define exbug(list) -> tailslist;
    vars item;
        [% until (tl(list) ->> item) = [] do
                item;
            enduntil; %] -> tailslist;
    enddefine;
```

Resources

Systems

POPLOG   University of Sussex
The dominant implementation of POP-11, which also includes DEC-10 Prolog, Common LISP and online documentation system. At the time of writing, available for DEC VAX/VMS, VAX Unix 4.2bsd, Sun Microsystems Sun-2 and Sun-3, Hewlett-Packard 9000-series, and Apollo systems. United Kingdom academic establishments should contact the University of Sussex; the United States academic sales contact is Computable Functions, Inc. Commercial sales are through Systems Designers.

Alpha POP-11   Cognitive Applications Limited
A newer and smaller system, developed for a wider market than POPLOG. Currently available for Apple Macintosh computers.

Books on POP-11

R. Barrett, A. Ramsay, A. Sloman, *POP-11: A Practical Language for Artificial Intelligence*, Ellis Horwood, 1985.
This was the first book published on POP-11: the authors are involved with POPLOG development.

R. Barrett, A. Ramsay, *Artificial Intelligence in Practice: Examples in POP-11*, Ellis Horwood, 1987.
A book of large example AI programs with sources in POP-11, based on research at the University of Sussex.

R. Burstall, Collins, R. Popplestone, *Programming in POP-2*, University Press, Edinburgh, 1968. Out of Print.
The original 'silver book'. POP-11 is close derivative of POP-2: most POP-11 systems have a compatibility library. This book contains mainly small procedures and their descriptions.

Burton, Shadbolt, *POP-11 Programming for Artificial Intelligence*, Addison-Wesley, 1987.

Artificial intelligence for cognitive psychologists, based on teaching material from the University of Nottingham.

M. Sharples, et al., *Computers and Thought* (Provisional title), MIT Press, scheduled Autumn 1987.
Based on teaching material from the Cognitive Studies Programme at the University of Sussex.

Further Reading

A. Aho, J. Ullman, *Principles of Compiler Design*, Addison-Wesley, 1977.
Everything you ever wanted to know about writing compilers.

J. Allen, *The Anatomy of LISP*,
Detailed coverage of the semantics of LISP systems.

M. Boden, *Artificial Intelligence and Natural Man*, Harvester 1977.
One of the great overviews of the field, giving a psychological and philosophical slant. Tremendous bibliography.

E. Charniak, D. McDermott, *Introduction to Artifical Intelligence*, Addison-Wesley, 1985.
A standard textbook on AI, with example programs in LISP. Includes work on vision.

W. Clocksin, C. Mellish, *Programming in PROLOG*, Springer-Verlag, 1981.
Standard textbook on PROLOG programming.

H. Dreyfus, *What Computers Can't Do: A Critique of Artificial Reason*, Harper and Row, 1972.
What computers might one day be able to do, from a philosophical point of view. Takes a negative view.

D. Knuth, *The Art of Computer Programming*, Vols. 1–3, Addison-Wesley, 1968–1981.
Everything you every wanted to know about computing, and then some. Especially good for data structures, numerical processing, sorting, assembler programming concepts.

Motorola, *MC68020 32-Bit Microprocessor User's Manual*, (2nd ed.), Prentice-Hall, 1985.
Detailed manual for 68000-family instruction set.

N. Nilsson, *Principles of Artificial Intelligence*, Tioga, 1980.
Serious approach to AI algorithms, with some proofs and complexity theory.

E. Rich, *Artificial Intelligence*, McGraw-Hill, 1983.
A standard textbook on AI. Includes a chapter on AI languages.

A. Sloman, *The Computer Revolution in Philosophy: Philosophy, Science, and Models of Mind*, Harvester 1978.
What computers might one day be able to do, from a philosophical point of view. Takes a positive view.

P. Winston, B. Horn, *LISP* (2nd ed.), Addison-Wesley, 1984.
A standard text on LISP programming. The second edition uses Common LISP.

User Groups

PLUG   POPLOG User Group
Secretary: Martin Bennett, Cambridge Consultants.

POP FORUM   Bulletin Board
Organiser: Steve Knight, Hewlett-Packard Labs, Bristol.
JANET address: **popforum@uk.co.hp.lb**

Contacts

Cambridge Consultants Ltd   Martin Bennett
The Science Park, Milton Road, Cambridge CB4 4DW. Phone (0223) 358855.
   Consultancy, training, PLUG; also market special object-oriented and real-time
   POP-11 toolkits.

Cognitive Applications Ltd   Alex Morrison
4 Sillwood Terrace, Brighton BN1 2LR. Phone (0273) 821600.
   Markets Alpha POP-11, consultancy, training.

Computable Functions, Inc   Robin Popplestone
United States. Phone (413) 545 3140
   POPLOG academic USA sales contact and Alpha POP-11 US distributor;
   consultancy, training.

GLH Limited   Jonathan Laventhol
7 Old Steine, Brighton BN1 1EJ. Phone (0273) 676688
   Consultancy, training.

Hewlett-Packard Research Laboratories   Steve Knight
Filton Road, Stoke Gifford, Bristol BS12 6QZ. Phone (0272) 799910.
   Organises POP FORUM.

Systems Designers   Alan Montgomery
Pembroke House, Pembroke Broadway, Camberley, Surrey GU15 3XD. Phone
(0276) 686200.
  Markets POPLOG, consultancy, training. Has offices in Europe and USA.

University of Sussex   Alan Johnson
Arts Block E, Falmer, Brighton BN1 9QN. Phone (0273) 606755.
  POPLOG developers, UK academic sales.

Index